ESSENTIAL FLAVORS

VIKING

Essential Flavors

The Simple Art of Cooking with Infused Oils, Flavored Vinegars, Essences, and Elixirs

Leslie Brenner & Katharine Kinsolving

VIKING
Published by the Penguin Group
Penguin Books USA Inc., 375 Hudson Street,
New York, New York 10014, U.S.A.
Penguin Books Ltd, 27 Wrights Lane, London W8 5TZ, England
Penguin Books Australia Ltd, Ringwood,Victoria, Australia
Penguin Books Canada Ltd, 10 Alcorn Avenue,
Toronto, Ontario, Canada M4V 3B2
Penguin Books (N.Z.) Ltd, 182-190 Wairau Road,
Auckland 10, New Zealand

Penguin Books Ltd, Registered Offices:
Harmondsworth, Middlesex, England

First published in 1994 by Viking Penguin,
a division of Penguin Books USA Inc.

10 9 8 7 6 5 4 3 2 1

PUBLISHER'S NOTE
The recipes contained in this book are to be followed exactly as written.
The Publisher is not responsible for addressing specific allergy and
other health needs which may require medical supervision. The
Publisher cannot be held responsible for any adverse
reactions to the recipes contained in this book.

LIBRARY OF CONGRESS CATALOGING-IN-PUBLICATION DATA
Brenner, Leslie.
Essential flavors: the simple art of cooking with infused oils,
flavored vinegars, essences, and elixirs/ Leslie Brenner
 and Katharine Kinsolving.
p.   cm.
Includes index.
ISBN 0–670–85523–5
1. Spices.   2. Flavoring essences.   3. Oils and fats, Edible.
4. Cookery (Vinegar)   I. Kinsolving, Katherine.   II. Title.
TX406.B7   1994
641.6′382—dc20   94–4215

Printed in the United States of America
Set in Adobe Simoncini Garamond
Designed by Cheryl L. Cipriani
Illustrations by Kathryn Parise

ACKNOWLEDGMENTS

We would like to extend our deepest thanks to our editor, Dawn Drzal, for her vision, encouragement, and unflagging energy all the way through this project; also for introducing us, taking us out to lunch when our spirits were low, giving us direction when we lost our way, testing recipes, chopping onions, stirring risotto, and peeling cherry tomatoes. Dawn, you're the editor of our dreams!

Thanks also to Beena Kamlani for her energy, good humor, and meticulous attention to detail, and to Bonnie Richmond of Cornell University for her advice on food safety issues.

THE AUTHORS

Thank you to Thierry Pérémarti, my adorable helpmeet; Jennifer Rudolph Walsh, my adorable agent; An-My Lê and Chris Fodor for their palates and support; John Brenner for his advice; Kimberly Charles for perfectly timed comic relief; and above all, Katy Kinsolving, who has made every day on this project a pleasure.

L. B.

Thank you to: Tasters above and beyond the call of duty, Mary and Lucien Kinsolving, Lucie Kinsolving and Dick McElhiney, and Lindsay and Markley Boyer; Jolie Hammer and Charlie Kinsolving for driving two hundred miles from one five-course meal to the next in walnut-oil country; and Amy Mastrangelo for encouragement and help with the cake solution. Finally, I want to thank my co-author—for enthusiasm even when concepts didn't work out, tremendous generosity with praise, unerring food instincts, and a personal style and warmth that pervade this book. And thanks for doing the fish.

I dedicate my half of this book to Rich Baumann, the essential ingredient in my life.

K. K.

CONTENTS

DISHES BY COURSE

Pastas and Risottos

Main Dishes

Complements

Desserts

ESSENTIAL FLAVORS

Introduction

All across the United States, cutting-edge chefs—from Jean-Georges Vongerichten, David Bouley, and Gray Kunz in New York to Michel Richard in Los Angeles—have been looking for ways to maximize the flavor in their dishes while relying less on the fat and flour that have long served as the underpinnings for traditional French cooking. Many of them have arrived at the same conclusion: that using flavor-infused oils and vinegars, concentrated vegetable pastes, and reduced stocks is the easiest way to achieve clean, pure, distilled flavors that excite the palate and provide substance to dishes in brand-new, more health-conscious ways.

Essential Flavors: The Simple Art of Cooking with Infused Oils, Flavored Vinegars, Essences, and Elixirs celebrates this new approach to spotlighting flavor and brings it into your kitchen at home. It is an approach that anyone who cooks can appreciate, because it saves time—not just for four-star chefs but also for those of us who throw together a bowl of pasta after a long day of work. *Essential Flavors* will change the way you think about ingredients, technique, and your time at the stove.

The concept is this: Make one or two herb- or fruit-infused oils or vinegars, a concentrated vegetable essence, and a vegetable- or wine-based broth or elixir on a lazy weekend. Most of them will take less than half an hour of your time in the kitchen to prepare; these flavor-packed essences do most of the work for you. The twenty-four hours the basil spends steeping in olive oil, for instance, is twenty-four hours of time you don't have to spend in the kitchen—the herbs and the oil work to create the essential flavor while you do something else. Use your new ingredients as instant flavorings to spruce up weekday salads, to perk up pastas, or in more sophisticated meals for company. With just a few of these oils, vinegars, essences, and elixirs in your refrigerator, you will have what we call a Pantry of Potential.

The beautiful part of this new wave of cooking is that once you've made an infused oil, flavored vinegar, essence, or elixir, it's a snap to whip up an original, elegant dish featuring it—either by following one of the dozens of recipes in the second part of this book or by using our recipes as springboards to inspire your own improvisations.

Essential Flavors breaks down into two parts. Part I, which includes the first three chapters, explains all you need to know about how to prepare the infused oils, flavored vinegars, essences, and elixirs. Chapter One leads you through the basics of making infused oils, Chapter Two will introduce you to the joy of flavoring your own vinegars, and Chapter Three demystifies essences and elixirs and shows how easy it is to make them.

Part II explains how to use your Pantry of Potential. It starts with "Openers," including soups and appetizers; then moves on to "Salads," including appetizer salads, main-dish salads, side-dish salads, and after-main-dish salads; "Pastas and Risottos," for flavor-driven carbo fixes; "Main Dishes," whether they be fish, poultry, or meat; "Complements," a collection of side dishes, including vegetable dishes, starches, and legumes; and, of course, "Desserts." The recipes in these chapters run the gamut from the simplest of the simple (such as Striped Bass Steamed with Ginger Oil and Scallions or Orecchiette in Leek Elixir with Spinach) to dishes that you'll want to make for company on a weekend (perhaps Pork Medallions on a Bed of Parsnip Purée with Opal Basil Vinegar Sauce or Hearts of Polenta with Wine-Dark Tomato Sauce). Some of the dishes are less lean than others; we couldn't resist including Seared Filet Mignon with Shallot Oil and Raw Shallots, although you can always choose something along the lines of Lemon Sole Baked in Parchment with Lemon-Herb Oil and Parsley. Among desserts you'll find a tempting array—ranging all along the health spectrum—from a refreshing Mint-Infused Blackberry Ice or Peaches Poached in Port-Pepper-Sage Elixir to more sinful indulgences such as a heavenly Fig Essence and Pistachio Tart or a sublime Orange–Bittersweet Chocolate Soufflé.

How to Use This Book

To make things simple, we've never required more than one infused oil, flavored vinegar, essence, or elixir in each recipe, although there are places where variations may suggest more than one. Vinaigrettes are a particularly good area for combining an infused oil and a flavored vinegar—in Chapter Five, "Salads," you'll find a list of our favorite vinaigrettes, and here we do break our one-essence-only rule.

To use the book, start by making an infused oil or two that appeals to you, and maybe put up one or two vinegars. The oils, none of which steep longer than forty-eight hours, will be ready relatively quickly. Look at the "Applications" under the oil you've made to find a listing of all the recipes in the book that feature that oil as an ingredient. The flavored vinegars list "Applications" the same way.

Essences and elixirs can be made much more quickly than the infused oils and flavored vinegars, many in less than half an hour. And some may be prepared while you're making another part of the dish, so you won't have to plan ahead. You can even jump right in and prepare a recipe using one of these tonight!

For the sake of convenience, you'll find the recipe for the oil, vinegar, essence, or elixir repeated, in shortened form, right alongside the recipes that use them, eliminating the inconvenience of flipping back and forth between sections.

Once you have a few infused oils, flavored vinegars, essences, and elixirs made up, you'll want to expand your collection and create another infused oil or flavored vinegar whenever the mood strikes you or should you happen to stumble across an ingredient that you don't often see. Say you happen to be in Chinatown and find fresh lemon grass—grab a big bunch, and take the opportunity to capture all that wonderful lemon-grass flavor in the Lemon Grass–Star Anise Vinegar.

This will get you started, but don't stop with our recipes. Once you've made a few, you'll see that *Essential Flavors* represents a whole new way of thinking about ingredients and flavors that readily lends itself to invention or to adding one of these new essences to recipes you've already grown to love.

A Note on Ingredients

What we cook can only be as good as the ingredients we use, so do take special care in selecting them.

For vegetables and fruits, buy what's fresh and in season. Really look at whatever you're buying, even pick it up and smell it—a pear should smell like a pear! If you're frustrated with cardboard string beans, Styrofoam tomatoes, and wooden peaches, take advantage of one of the farmers' markets that are sprouting up all over the country. You'll not only find flavorful ripe tomatoes in season and bounteous supplies of the best herbs, you'll also be introduced to a wider variety of "heirloom" fruits and vegetables, unusual herbs and tubers, and just-picked baby lettuces. Organic produce (much of which can be found at the farmers' markets) tends to have the best flavor—it really tastes like what it's supposed to taste like—and of course by savoring organic produce, we can discourage the use of pesticides and thus help reduce the threats they pose to our health and the environment. If your supermarket doesn't carry organic produce, ask the management to start—it's surprising how quickly they'll respond to demand.

Try to buy locally grown produce whenever possible. Remember that those imported yellow peppers or that out-of-season asparagus must be flown long distances, and jet-fuel emissions aren't the greatest thing for the environment either. Happily, the proliferation of farmers' markets has improved the economic climate for small farmers. Supporting them is a way of sending a message that we care about what we consume and how it's grown.

Make an effort to buy organically raised meats and free-range, organically raised poultry. They're more healthful and more flavorful as well.

Buy the freshest fish you can find, and for safety reasons, pay attention to how it's displayed. It should be well iced and not touching any cooked foods. The eyes on whole fish should be clear, and fish shouldn't give off any "fishy" smell. (Don't be embarrassed to ask to smell it!) The best bet is to find a fishmonger you trust and become a regular customer. It's difficult in most areas to find very fresh fish on Sundays, since the big wholesale fishmarkets are closed, so plan accordingly!

Since salt is such a ubiquitous ingredient, why not use a good one? We prefer sea salt to regular iodized salt, which has a faintly chemical taste. Kosher salt works nicely, too. And never use pre-ground pepper, which becomes bitter and picks up off-tastes rather quickly. We like to have two pepper grinders on hand in the kitchen—one filled with high-quality whole black peppercorns such as Malabar, Tellicherry, or Sarawak and the other filled with white peppercorns. When we call for "freshly ground pepper" in a recipe without specifying black or white, that means either would be fine, depending on your taste and what you have on hand. The French, incidentally, tend to use freshly ground white pepper more routinely than Americans do; it is more subtly spicy than black pepper.

As for wines used in cooking, a good general rule is that if you wouldn't drink it, don't cook with it. On the other hand, don't spend a lot of money on wines you'll be cooking with, since you'll lose the subtleties of the wine anyway. Look for what's on special at your wine shop. For dry white cooking wines, California or Australian sauvignon blancs will do the trick handily; for reds, inexpensive French Bordeaux or pinot noirs from California, Washington State, or Oregon are good bets. We've found that on the East Coast, French wines are a much better buy than on the West Coast, and California wines are pretty expensive. Obviously, on the West Coast California wines prevail.

In recipes using port, look for ruby port (as distinguished from tawny port, which is aged longer in oak and has a different character than ruby). Choose an inexpensive one, but if you're not sure about the label, do choose one from Portugal and you'll be safe. Do not choose one of the very cheap ports from California or New York State or you may run the risk of ruining your sauce.

Many of our recipes call for chicken stock. Homemade is obviously better than canned, though in certain cases we provide an alternative, which is to dilute canned broth with a little water. Though you'll taste the difference more in some types of recipes than others, do consider taking up the habit of making your own stock if you don't already.

All our recipes use large eggs. We find that organically grown eggs are fresher and superior in flavor.

For desserts, we've developed and tested all our chocolate recipes using Lindt Excellence, a Swiss bittersweet chocolate that is widely available in three-ounce bars and that we find to be delicious, with a marvelous smooth texture. High-quality bittersweet chocolates, such as Valrhona or Callebaut, or most Swiss bittersweet chocolates would be fine substitutes.

For flour, use unbleached all-purpose white flour.

When butter is called for, always use fresh unsalted (also called "sweet") butter, which allows you much better control over the final amount of salt in a recipe. Unsalted butter doesn't stay fresh as long as salted, but you can freeze it and thaw just as you need it.

PART ONE

The Pantry of Potential

Infused Oils, Flavored Vinegars, Essences, and Elixirs

What They Are and How to Make Them

Bottles of brightly colored *infused oils* and *flavored vinegars* line our Pantry of Potential, all rich with strains of fresh fruit, exotic spices, and bunches of herbs from the farmers' market. These beautiful bottles stand at attention on our shelves, their contents ready to be whisked into lively vinaigrettes, added to pan sauces, or drizzled over grilled fish. The pantry also includes thick purées of common vegetables and fruits, which we have roasted or cooked, capturing their essential flavors in the process. We call them *essences* and use them sparingly, a few tablespoons at a time, to coat a roast or to stir into a soup. Finally, it holds a number of magical concoctions, simple to make but sublime to taste. We refer to them as *elixirs,* because they bring new life to familiar fare. Some of these elixirs are water-based infusions—flavorful broths made by steeping mushrooms or peppermint leaves in water. Others are alcohol-based and more sophisticated. Not only have these four new ingredients—infused oils, flavored vinegars, essences, and elixirs—transformed the way we cook and eat, they are also a snap to make.

An infused oil or flavored
vinegar packaged in a
striking bottle naturally
makes a wonderful gift from
the heart, filled with flavor
from the kitchen.
Houseware and kitchen
stores often stock a large
variety of decorative bottles.
They're also available
through many of the mail-
order kitchen supply
sources, such as Williams-
Sonoma—or try your local
flea market. For infused oils
or flavored vinegars with a
particularly gorgeous color,
whether it be the peridot
green of Chive Oil or the
deep violet of Blackberry
Vinegar, you'll want clear
glass to show off what's
inside; for others you might
want cobalt blue or pale
green tinted glass. If the
bottles don't come with
corks, pick up new ones by
the dozen at kitchen supply
or hardware stores.

Once a bottle is filled for
gift giving, make sure it is
corked very tightly, tie a
generous bow around the
neck, and add a small label
or tag with the name of the
oil or vinegar and a note
identifying its expiration
date (for oils, two to three
weeks after bottling;
vinegars last from six

Most important, these new ingredients are quickly prepared. Steal ten minutes from your day to heat up a bit of
chopped ginger and a cup of oil in a saucepan, and then pour
them into a jar to steep—the ingredients do the work while
you go off to bed or to the office or the movies. The next day,
or even the day after, when you strain the contents and put
your new bottle of Ginger Oil into the refrigerator, you will
have started *your* Pantry of Potential. Even if you have only
one infused oil on hand, that one is enough to add a sparkle
to a midweek supper. Or snatch five minutes to combine a
pint of ripe blackberries with a couple of cups of vinegar, and
then put them aside for a couple of weeks so that the vinegar
and the berries marry before joining your pantry.

Essences, those thick concentrations of flavor, may take a
bit more kitchen time, but most of that is roasting or simmering time, which leaves you free to do something else. How
easy it is to slide a tray of tomatoes into a slow oven and forget about them for a couple of hours while you attend to
other matters in the kitchen or help the kids with their home-
work! When the timer dings two hours later, the tomatoes
are roasted through—sweet and soft, concentrated in flavor.
All you have to do is give them a whirl in the food processor
and pack them away in the refrigerator for use some night
later in the week, when time is of the essence; or freeze them
and pull them out in the dark of winter, when there isn't a
ripe tomato in sight.

Elixirs often involve no more time than the ten minutes it
takes to boil a kettle of water. Others require a little more
time but can simmer on the back burner while dinner is being made.

The purpose of these new ingredients is to save time,
while bringing back the old-fashioned home-cooked flavor
we all yearn for.

The Flavors

Herbs have a starring role: most of the infused oils and flavored vinegars take their essential flavors from them.

For the infused oils, we use basil, mint, rosemary, thyme, chives, and tarragon. The first four—basil, mint, rosemary, and thyme—are all members of the same botanical family, Labiatae. All Labiatae herbs carry essential oils in their leaves and stems, oils that meld beautifully with the oils they're infusing. (They also suspend wonderfully to flavor the vinegars, where opal basil, mint, and thyme are used as well.)

Chives, the brightest-tasting member of the onion family, also make an appearance in the infused oils. (Picture Chive Oil drizzled over mashed potatoes!) Tarragon, the only kitchen herb from the daisy family, has long been used to flavor vinegars, but we've also used it to infuse one of our favorite oils.

Sage, which in days of old was purported to have mystical properties and bestow wisdom, is the essential flavor for one of our loveliest vinegars. Another calls for fresh lemon grass, a lively Southeast Asian herb that can be found in many Asian groceries.

For the infused oils and flavored vinegars, use fresh herbs—dried won't work. If you're lucky enough to have an herb garden or window box of your own, you can be sure of the quality; otherwise try to find organically grown herbs. Though many supermarkets now carry a good selection, you may find fresher herbs, and a larger selection, at your local farmers' market. Select herbs that are bright in color, with leaves that are unblemished, not wilted, and not falling off the stems. Thyme should be young, without woody-looking stems. Rosemary needles should be supple. Try to taste a sample before purchasing, and make sure it has a nice strong punch. Herbs can vary greatly in intensity from batch to

months to a year). Although the flavorings have been removed, you may want to add a pretty branch of thyme to the Thyme Oil, rosemary to the Rosemary Oil, or tarragon to the Pink Tarragon Vinegar, just for show. Also be sure to add a tag with instructions for storing: oils should say something like "Refrigerate me!" and vinegars should say "Store in a cool, dark place."

Finding Fresh Herbs

Fresh herbs, including opal basil, lemon grass, sage, and all other herbs called for in this book, are available through mail-order sources such as Aux Delices Des Bois. Call (800) 666-1232, or fax (212) 334-1231. Herbs are sold by the ounce, and are subject to availability.

batch, and that will, of course, affect your oil. We've sampled some "tarragon" that we think may have been grass! You might want to increase the amount of herbs by half during the winter months—the flavor of fresh herbs is just not as deep when the sun isn't shining.

Spices infuse several oils and flavor one of the vinegars.

The warmth of cumin suffuses one oil; another gets its essential flavor from curry. We like our spices toasted, and we describe how to do so quickly and easily in the recipes. Cumin is available in both seed and powdered form. If you have a spice grinder, we suggest that you buy your cumin in seed form and grind it yourself for a nuttier flavor. The powdered version tends to lose its potency sooner than the seeds. Curry is an all-encompassing name for a number of magical spice mixtures. The type of curry you use is a matter of individual taste—some like it very hot, others prefer a milder version. Use your favorite—toasted, if you like.

Pink peppercorns (which are actually unrelated to true pepper) flavor the Lime Pink Peppercorn Oil. Find them at gourmet and specialty-food shops—look for unbroken, deep-rose-colored peppercorns. Several recipes in Part II call for them as well, so be sure to get a good supply.

Star anise makes an appearance in Lemon Grass–Star Anise Vinegar (as well as in one of the elixirs). This handsome spice may be found in both Asian and Latin American markets, as it's used in both types of cuisines. Look for unbroken, unshriveled stars.

Fruits are used in all four types of essential flavors.

Citrus—lemon, lime, and orange—infuses three of the oils, orange by itself and the others in combination.

The flavored vinegars use blackberries and plums. Since both have limited seasons, buy the fruit at its peak and consider doubling the recipe for year-round use.

Plums also form the base for one of the elixirs; figs show up in a luxurious essence.

$\mathcal{R}$oots—such as ginger, shallots, and garlic—provide the essential flavor for a number of the infused oils, flavored vinegars, and essences.

Ginger is available in many forms—powdered, candied, and pickled—but you'll need to find it in its fresh, natural state. If the grocer doesn't have it, look in an Asian market. It's an ornery-looking root that wanders along, branching off here and there. Peel it with a small, sharp paring knife before you chop, and remember that the finer you chop it, the more flavorful your oil will be.

Shallots—our favorite member of the allium (onion) family, mild and lovely with a sophisticated flavor all their own—provide the essential flavor for one of the infused oils and one of the essences. If you can't find them in your supermarket, ask the grocer to order them for you. Do not substitute onions or scallions (sometimes called green onions) for shallots in the oil or essence. If you live in a part of the country where it's absolutely impossible to get them, use white (not yellow or Spanish) onions in the recipes in Part II. The size of shallots, which grow in cloves like garlic, varies widely, and we've noticed that on the East Coast they're much larger than they are on the West Coast. When we call for a shallot we mean a medium-size one, which is about triple the size of an average garlic clove. (For simplicity's sake, we've given a tablespoon or cup equivalent for chopped shallots.)

Finally, no collection of infused oils would be complete without a garlic-infused oil. However, we find raw garlic too harsh for this use, so we've described how to roast the garlic before combining it with the oil. The result is heavenly and unctuous; the sweet and subtle taste of Roasted-Garlic Oil will convert even those who turn up their noses at garlic.

CHAPTER ONE

Infused Oils

M aking an infused oil is no more complicated than making a cup of tea. When you make a cup of tea, you heat the water, add the tea, and steep it; pretty soon, the water has been *infused* with the flavor from the tea leaves. The principle is the same for infused oil: You combine the oil with an herb, a spice, or an aromatic vegetable or fruit of your choosing and let them steep together in the refrigerator for 24 to 48 hours. The oil is then *infused* with the flavor of the ingredient you have chosen.

The exciting thing about infused oils is their versatility. To think of an infused oil only as an ingredient in a vinaigrette would be a crime. We use them, with delicious results, in a variety of applications: drizzled onto steamed fish or roasted potatoes, in pasta dishes, in vegetable purées—even in desserts. And the list doesn't end there. Of course, they do have their limitations: Generally speaking we do not use them for sautéing or frying because high direct heat tends to break down their flavor. Cooking methods using ambient heat, such as roasting or baking, however, work very nicely.

Important Instructions

There are three important general guidelines to follow when making the infused oils:

1. As with any culinary preparation, make sure that all ingredients are fresh and clean. All containers—saucepans, funnels, jars, and so on—must be extremely clean as well. Sterilize them if you feel you should. And all counters must also be clean. If you have any doubt about the freshness of any ingredient or the cleanliness of any utensil, don't use it.

2. Do not let the oils get too hot or they will fry the ingredients; when we say "warm gently," use the lowest heat possible. The purpose of the heat is not to cook the ingredients but rather to help release their essential oils. Note that in making some of the oils (specifically Mint Oil), the oil does not need to be heated at all.

3. It is necessary to refrigerate the oils while they are steeping (24 to 48 hours), and you *must* store them refrigerated once they're infused. (Storage below 45°F. slows rancidity and prevents growth of anaerobic bacteria.) Label each oil with the contents and the date it was made. The infused oils should keep in the refrigerator for two to three weeks.

Kitchen Equipment Needed for Making Infused Oils

A blender or food processor: While you may not need this for every oil, some of the herb-infused oils benefit from a whirl in the blender or food processor. The blades cut the herbs into smaller pieces, creating a stronger infusion.

A collection of 16-ounce glass jars with lids: Mason jars work nicely, but we have also used old jam, mustard, and mayonnaise jars. You may want to store the oils in smaller jars or in tightly corked glass bottles for easy pouring. The jars, lids, and bottles should be as clean as possible; sterilizing them is safest.

A small kitchen funnel: Those with a short stem and a large bowl work best.

Paper coffee filters (the conical type) and a clean pastry brush: Buy or locate your funnel first, then buy coffee filters in a size that will fit snugly into it. The paper filters soak up oil, so we have added an additional teaspoon of plain oil to each recipe. Paint this onto the filter with the pastry brush before the oil is strained. Because the filter is then fully saturated with the plain oil, it will not soak up your precious infused oil.

Masking tape and an indelible marker for labeling the jars: Once you have strained an infused oil into its final jar, you should label it to identify the oil and record the day it was made. Masking tape is the easiest and cheapest way of labeling we know. If you can find them, get a few Sharpie markers—they'll write on anything!

Ingredients for Infused Oils

Oil: The oil you use will have a tremendous impact on the finished product. First and foremost, the oil should be absolutely fresh. If you detect even a hint of rancidity, discard it. Never use a recycled oil that you have used for some other purpose (such as frying) to make an infused oil. We store all our oils in the refrigerator, even before infusing them, to prevent rancidity.

Many of the infused-oil recipes call for a base of canola oil or safflower oil. Both are flavorless and will not compete with the ingredients flavoring them; they're widely available in grocery stores; and they're the two most healthful oils because they contain the lowest percentage of saturated fatty acids. Corn and peanut oil, which are perfectly fine for many culinary preparations, are not suitable bases for infused oils because of their stronger flavors.

Other infused oils in this chapter are made with a base of extra-virgin olive oil, or with a combination of canola oil or safflower oil and extra-virgin olive oil. We've found that certain ingredients—rosemary, roasted garlic, and shallots, to name a few—benefit from the backbone of a fruity extra-virgin olive oil.

Volumes have been written about how to choose an extra-virgin olive oil, but briefly, look for a bright yellow or yellow-green color, and a fresh (not overpowering) fruity or slightly olive-y aroma, with no hint of rancidity. (You may have to sample a small bottle or two before you find one you like.) We do specify "extra-virgin" olive oil rather than "virgin" or "pure." Extra-virgin is the product of the first pressing of the olives, and as a result, it has a finer, more complex character than the products of the subsequent extractions. Those labeled "virgin" or "pure" are allowed a higher percentage of free oleic acid, which imparts a harshness to the oil. Those who don't like olive oil because it's too "strong" are probably reacting to those with higher percentages of these acids. While a virgin olive oil is allowed 4 percent oleic acid, extra-virgin is allowed only 1 percent.

On the other hand, don't go overboard and spend twenty dollars on a "designer" bottle—the subtle nuances on which such an olive oil prides itself will be hidden by the herbs infusing it. Five to ten dollars for half a liter should be the appropriate range in most areas of the country.

Keep in mind that besides the Mediterranean lands—Italy, Spain, southern France, and Greece—California and Australia are also producing a number of good olive oils. In any case, we know extra-virgin olive oil is liquid gold, so where we have called for a quantity of it, you can be sure that the results will merit the cost.

A word about other oils: There are a number of other "specialty" oils on the market. For the most part they are made from nuts and seeds and have wonderful rich flavors in and of themselves. Hazelnut oil, walnut oil, almond oil, and sesame oil, for example, are much-used ingredients in our pantry, especially when combined with flavored vinegars. All these oils should be kept refrigerated; they are quite perishable and may turn rancid if they are kept at room temperature. A few of the recipes in Part II call for them, and we encourage you to experiment. Just remember, they are very dense in flavor—a well-placed tablespoon will go a long way!

We have also noted with pleasure the recent introduction of commercially produced flavored and essential oils onto the market. Use caution if you are planning to substitute a commercially made flavored oil for one of the infused oils we describe. They vary greatly in intensity, and while some may work beautifully, others may be too strong or not strong enough. Commercially made chili oils, for example, can be wickedly hot, so start with a very small amount. The pure oils of oranges, lemons, and limes, packaged by Boyajian, among others, and available at Williams-Sonoma and other specialty-food stores, are oil extracts pressed from the skins of these fruits. They are very, very strong and meant to be used instead of the zest of the fruit. They are not similar to, and cannot be substituted for, any of our citrus-infused oils.

Infusors: Once you have the equipment and the oil selected and ready to go, turn your attention to what you will steep in the oil.

To repeat, all ingredients should be fresh and clean. This is important, as oil is a favorite medium for bacteria.

Most of the recipes call for one or two ounces of fresh herbs. In our experience, most herbs are wrapped and sold in one-ounce bundles, but double-check when you make your purchase. We have included rough cup measurements for those of you growing herbs at home. To prepare the herbs, discard any blackened or wilted leaves and wash the remaining leaves gently in cold water. To dry the herbs, lay them out on a piece of toweling, or spin them dry in a salad spinner. Don't wring them out in a towel or you'll lose some of the essential herb flavor that you want to infuse your oil!

Citrus fruit: First, wash the fruit—we use warm water and a little mild dish soap. Be sure to rinse carefully and dry. (Wash just before using or the peel will shrivel.) The key to creating oils infused with citrus is in how you peel the zest away from the fruit. The zest (the colored part of the peel) is the part of the fruit that carries all the flavorful essential oils that you want to transfer to your jar of vegetable oil. Beneath the zest lies the bitter white pith, which should be avoided, as it adds a distasteful harshness. We have found that using a good, sharp vegetable peeler makes it very easy to peel away the zest, leaving the nasty old pith behind.

Without further ado, then, here are the Infused Oils. . . .

Thyme Oil

2 small bunches thyme (about 1 ounce each), rinsed and dried
1⅓ cups extra-virgin olive oil
1 teaspoon canola oil or safflower oil

1. Break up the thyme (no need to remove the leaves from the stems) and bruise it by smashing it with a mallet, rolling pin, or other heavy object. Place the thyme in a small saucepan, cover with the olive oil, and warm gently for 6 to 7 minutes. Pour into a very clean jar, let cool, cover, and let steep in the refrigerator for 24 to 48 hours.

2. Line a funnel with a paper coffee filter and use a pastry brush to paint the filter with the teaspoon of canola oil. Pour the Thyme Oil into the filter and let it drip through the funnel into a very clean jar or bottle (this will take several hours). Cover or cork tightly and label with the date. Store refrigerated.

MAKES JUST OVER 1 CUP.

Applications

Warmed Chèvre Salad with Sun-Dried Tomato Elixir (Variation)
Wild Mushroom Agnolotti with Thyme Oil
Pasta Pissaladière
Potato Purée with Thyme Oil
Fast-as-Lightning Minted Zucchini (Variation)
"Miracle" Cherry Tomatoes (Variation)

Baked Tomatoes with Cornbread Stuffing and Cumin Oil
(Variation)

Also see "Our Favorite Vinaigrettes," page 112, and "Our Favorite Weeknight Pastas," page 130.

Mint Oil

2 ounces fresh mint (about 2 cups leaves), rinsed, patted dry, and allowed to air-dry thoroughly
1 cup plus 1 teaspoon canola oil or safflower oil

1. After discarding the larger stalks from the mint, combine the leaves and the cup of oil in a food processor or blender and process or blend for 10 seconds. Pour into a very clean jar, cover, and let steep in the refrigerator for 24 to 48 hours.

2. Line a funnel with a paper coffee filter and use a pastry brush to paint the filter with the remaining teaspoon of oil. Pour the Mint Oil into the filter and let it drip through the funnel into another very clean jar or bottle (this may take some time). Cover or cork tightly and label with the date. Store refrigerated.

MAKES ABOUT 1 CUP.

Applications

Chilled Minted Tomato Soup
Minted Melon and Prosciutto
Fast-as-Lightning Minted Zucchini
Chocolate-Mint Chiffon Cake

Basil Oil

2½ to 3 cups loosely packed fresh basil leaves, rinsed
¾ cup extra-virgin olive oil
½ cup plus 1 teaspoon canola oil or safflower oil

1. Briefly dunk the basil leaves in boiling water and then plunge them into a bowl of ice water. Drain the basil and blot it with a paper towel to remove excess liquid.

2. Combine the basil, olive oil, and ½ cup of the canola oil in a saucepan and warm gently for 8 to 10 minutes. Remove to a food processor; process 30 seconds. Pour into a very clean jar, let cool, cover, and let steep in the refrigerator for 24 to 48 hours.

3. Line a funnel with a paper coffee filter and use a pastry brush to paint the filter with the remaining teaspoon of canola oil. Pour the Basil Oil into the filter and let it drip through the funnel into another very clean jar or bottle (this may take some time). Cover or cork tightly and label with the date. Store refrigerated.

MAKES ABOUT 1 CUP.

Applications

Colorful Grilled Chicken Salad on a Bed of Arugula with Basil Lime Vinaigrette

Fennel Salad with Roasted-Beet Essence and Orange Zest

Warmed Chèvre Salad with Sun-Dried Tomato Elixir (Variation)

Penne with Shrimp, Peas, Tomato Bits, and Basil Oil

Grilled Baby Eggplant with Basil Oil Vinaigrette

Fresh Tomato Salad with Chèvre and Rosemary Oil (Variation)

"Miracle" Cherry Tomatoes (Variation)

Potato Purée with Thyme Oil (Variation)

Also see "Our Favorite Vinaigrettes," page 112, and "Our Favorite Weeknight Pastas," page 130.

Essential Flavors

Tarragon Oil

**2 ounces fresh tarragon (about 3 cups leaves), rinsed and
    dried**
1 cup plus 1 teaspoon canola oil or safflower oil

1. Strip the tarragon leaves away from the larger stalks. Combine the leaves and the cup of oil in a saucepan. Gently heat to a bare simmer. Remove from heat and process in a food processor or blender for 10 seconds. Pour into a very clean jar, let cool, cover, and let steep in the refrigerator for 24 to 48 hours.

2. Line a funnel with a paper coffee filter and use a pastry brush to paint the filter with the remaining teaspoon of oil. Pour the Tarragon Oil into the filter and let it drip through the funnel into another very clean jar or bottle (this may take some time). Cover or cork tightly and label with the date. Store refrigerated.

MAKES ABOUT 1 CUP.

Applications

Carrot–Celery Root Salad with Tarragon Oil
"Miracle" Cherry Tomatoes
Leeks with Sage Vinaigrette (Variation)
Fresh Tomato Salad with Chèvre and Rosemary Oil
    (Variation)

Also see "Our Favorite Vinaigrettes," page 112.

Rosemary Oil

1 ounce fresh rosemary (about 1 cup leaves), rinsed and dried
1 cup extra-virgin olive oil
1 teaspoon canola oil or safflower oil

1. Strip the rosemary leaves from the stalks. Combine the leaves and the olive oil in a saucepan and warm gently for 5 to 7 minutes. Remove from the heat and process in a food processor or blender for 10 seconds. Pour into a very clean jar, let cool, cover, and let steep in the refrigerator for 24 to 48 hours.

2. Line a funnel with a paper coffee filter and use a pastry brush to paint the filter with the teaspoon of canola oil. Pour the Rosemary Oil into the filter and let it drip through the funnel into another very clean jar or bottle (this may take some time). Cover or cork tightly and label with the date. Store refrigerated.

MAKES ABOUT 1 CUP.

Applications

Fresh Tomato Salad with Chèvre and Rosemary Oil
Penne with Fresh and Wild Mushrooms and Rosemary Oil
Halibut with Rosemary Oil
Rosemary Citrus Cornbread
Chicken Breasts with Rosemary-Leek Coulis
Veal Scallops with Rosemary-Orange Sauce
White Beans with Rosemary Oil

Rosemary Potatoes "Sarladaise"
Rosemary-Oil Olive Country Bread
"Miracle" Cherry Tomatoes (Variation)
Potato Purée with Thyme Oil (Variation)

Also see "Our Favorite Vinaigrettes," page 112, and "Our Favorite Weeknight Pastas," page 130.

Chive Oil

1½ ounces fresh chives, chopped into ½-inch pieces (about 1½ cups)
1 cup plus 1 teaspoon canola oil or safflower oil

1. Combine the chives and the cup of oil in a saucepan and gently heat to a bare simmer. Remove from the heat, pour into a food processor or blender, and process for 10 seconds. Pour into a very clean jar, let cool, cover, and let steep in the refrigerator for 24 to 48 hours.

2. Line a funnel with a paper coffee filter and use a pastry brush to paint the filter with the remaining teaspoon of oil. Pour the Chive Oil into the filter and let it drip through the funnel into another very clean jar or bottle (this may take some time). Cover or cork tightly and label with the date. Store refrigerated.

MAKES ABOUT 1 CUP.

Applications

Endive and Orange Salad with Chive Oil

Soft-Shell Crabs with Citrus-Chive Sauce

Skate Steamed with Chive Oil and Lemon

Grilled Chicken Breasts with Roasted Red
     Pepper–Chive–Lime Sauce

Poached Sausages and Potatoes with Heavenly Vinaigrette

"Miracle" Cherry Tomatoes (Variation)

Potato Purée with Thyme Oil (Variation)

Also see "Our Favorite Vinaigrettes," page 112, and "Our Favorite Weeknight Pastas," page 130.

Orange-Infused Oil

Lovely and mild, not to be confused with commercially available orange oil.

2 oranges
1 cup plus 1 teaspoon canola oil or safflower oil

1. Using a vegetable peeler, peel the zest away from the two oranges, making sure to leave the bitter white pith on the orange. Cut the orange zest into thinner strips, put them into a saucepan with the cup of oil, and warm gently for 5 minutes. Remove to a very clean jar, let cool, cover, and let steep in the refrigerator for 24 to 48 hours.

2. Line a funnel with a paper coffee filter and use a pastry brush to paint the filter with the remaining teaspoon of oil. Pour the Orange-Infused Oil into the filter and let it drip through the funnel into another very clean jar or bottle (this may take some time). Cover or cork tightly and label with the date. Store refrigerated.

MAKES ABOUT 1 CUP.

Applications

Braised and Roasted Endives with Orange-Infused Oil
Potato Thimbles with Orange-Parsley Pesto
Orange–Bittersweet Chocolate Soufflé
Lemon-Ginger Cake (Variation)

Lime Pink Peppercorn Oil

4 limes
1½ tablespoons pink peppercorns, roughly crushed
1 cup plus 1 teaspoon canola oil or safflower oil

1. Using a vegetable peeler, peel the zest away from the limes, making sure to leave the bitter white pith on the limes. Cut the lime zest into thinner strips. Combine the strips of lime zest, the crushed pink peppercorns, and the cup of oil in a saucepan and warm gently for 5 minutes. Remove to a very clean jar, let cool, cover, and let steep in the refrigerator for 24 to 48 hours.

2. Line a funnel with a paper coffee filter and use a pastry brush to paint the filter with the remaining teaspoon of oil. Pour the Lime Pink Peppercorn Oil into the filter and let it drip through the funnel into another very clean jar or bottle (this may take some time). Cover or cork tightly and label with the date. Store refrigerated.

MAKES ABOUT 1 CUP.

Applications

Winter Vegetable Purée with Lime Pink Peppercorn Oil
Asparagus with Shallot Vinaigrette (Variation)

Also see "Our Favorite Vinaigrettes," page 112.

Lemon-Herb Oil

Thyme gives this lemony oil a complexity we love, yet it's softer than the Thyme Oil on page 24, since it uses canola oil or safflower oil as its base rather than olive oil. We use this in creations both savory and sweet.

1 lemon
1 ounce fresh thyme
1 cup plus 1 teaspoon canola oil or safflower oil

1. With a vegetable peeler, peel the yellow zest from the lemon, making sure to leave the white pith on the fruit. Wash the thyme, then break it up and "bruise" it using a mallet, rolling pin, or other heavy object. Put the thyme in a saucepan with the lemon zest and the cup of oil. Warm gently over low heat for 5 minutes. Pour into a very clean jar, let cool, cover, and let steep in the refrigerator for 24 to 48 hours.

2. Line a funnel with a paper coffee filter and use a pastry brush to paint the filter with the remaining teaspoon of oil. Pour the Lemon-Herb Oil into the filter and let it drip through the funnel into another very clean jar or bottle (this may take some time). Cover or cork tightly and label with the date. Store refrigerated.

MAKES ABOUT 1 CUP.

Applications

Sweet Pea Soup Kissed with Lemon
Grilled Tuna with Lemon-Herb Oil and Tomato-Olive
    Concasse

Lemon Sole Baked in Parchment with Lemon-Herb Oil and Parsley

New Potatoes Roasted with Lemon-Herb Oil and Bay Leaves

Lemon-Ginger Cake (Variation)

Essential Flavors

Curry Oil

In Indian cooking, spices are often dry-roasted in the pan to bring out the flavors just before using. We've found that some people prefer the deeper, almost nutty flavor that roasting imparts to curry; others like the brighter flavor of raw curry. But you decide, and use your favorite curry powder (ours is Madras —a pretty hot one) for a personalized oil.

3 tablespoons curry powder
1 cup plus 1 teaspoon canola oil or safflower oil

1. Place the curry powder in a small saucepan or skillet and, if desired, warm gently for 3 to 4 minutes, or until the curry aromas start to announce themselves.

2. Whether you've roasted the curry or not, add the cup of oil and warm gently for 4 minutes. Pour into a very clean jar, let cool, cover, and let steep in the refrigerator for 24 to 48 hours. Line a funnel with a paper coffee filter and use a pastry brush to paint the filter with the remaining teaspoon of oil. Pour the Curry Oil into the filter and let it drip through the funnel into a very clean jar or bottle (this will take several hours). Cover or cork tightly and label with the date. Store refrigerated.

MAKES ABOUT 1 CUP.

Applications

Grilled Shrimp with Curry Oil
Spinach Sautéed with Curry Oil
Potato Purée with Thyme Oil (Variation)

Cumin Oil

**3 tablespoons cumin seeds or 3 tablespoons packaged
ground cumin**
1 cup plus 1 teaspoon canola oil or safflower oil

1. If you are using cumin seeds, roast them over moderate
heat in a dry sauté pan for 2 to 3 minutes, grind them in a
spice grinder or mini-chop or with a mortar and pestle,
and then combine with the cup of oil and gently warm for
5 minutes.

   or

   If you are using packaged ground cumin, measure the
cumin into a dry, heavy-bottomed saucepan. Gently roast
the ground cumin for about 2 minutes over medium heat
to release its aroma, then add the cup of oil and gently
warm for 5 minutes.

2. Pour into a very clean jar, let cool, cover, and let steep in
the refrigerator for 24 to 48 hours. Line a funnel with a
paper coffee filter and use a pastry brush to paint the filter
with the remaining teaspoon of oil. Pour the Cumin Oil
into the filter and let it drip through the funnel into another very clean jar or bottle (this may take some time).
Cover or cork tightly and label with the date. Store refrigerated.

MAKES ABOUT 1 CUP.

Applications

Baked Tomatoes with Cornbread Stuffing and Cumin Oil
Roasted Potatoes and Shallots with Cumin Oil
Rice Pilaf with Cumin Oil and Cilantro
Spinach Sautéed with Curry Oil (Variation)

Ginger Oil

**one 4-inch piece ginger root, peeled and chopped into
small dice**
1 cup plus 1 teaspoon canola oil or safflower oil

1. Combine the ginger and the cup of oil in a saucepan and
   warm gently for 10 to 12 minutes. Pour into a very clean
   jar, let cool, cover, and let steep in the refrigerator for 24
   to 48 hours.

2. Line a funnel with a paper coffee filter and use a pastry
   brush to paint the filter with the remaining teaspoon
   of oil. Pour the Ginger Oil into the filter and let it drip
   through the funnel into another very clean jar or bottle
   (this may take some time). Cover or cork tightly and label
   with the date. Store refrigerated.

MAKES ABOUT 1 CUP.

Applications

Shrimp with Black Beans, Lime, and Ginger Oil
Striped Bass Steamed with Ginger Oil and Scallions
Lime Ginger Couscous
Gingery Apple Pie
Hazelnut Ginger Pear Tarte "Tatin"
Lemon-Ginger Cake
Winter Vegetable Purée with Lime Pink Peppercorn Oil
  (Variation)
Chocolate-Mint Chiffon Cake (Variation)

Also see "Our Favorite Vinaigrettes," page 112.

Shallot Oil

10 shallots, sliced
½ cup plus 1 teaspoon canola oil or safflower oil
½ cup extra-virgin olive oil

1. Combine the shallots, ½ cup canola oil, and the olive oil in a saucepan and gently heat to a bare simmer. Remove from the heat and pour into a clean jar, let cool, cover, and let steep in the refrigerator for 24 to 48 hours.

2. Line a funnel with a paper coffee filter and use a pastry brush to paint the filter with the remaining teaspoon of canola oil. Pour the Shallot Oil into the filter and let it drip through the funnel into another very clean jar or bottle (this may take some time). Cover or cork tightly and label with the date. Store refrigerated.

MAKES ABOUT 1 CUP.

Applications

Roast Portobello Mushrooms with Porcini Elixir
Asparagus with Shallot Vinaigrette
Bistro Salad
Poached Sausages and Potatoes with Heavenly Vinaigrette
Flank Steak Marinated in Plum Vinegar
Seared Filet Mignon with Shallot Oil and Raw Shallots
Roasted-Carrot Purée
Roasted Potatoes and Shallots with Cumin Oil (Variation)

Baked Tomatoes with Cornbread Stuffing and Cumin Oil
(Variation)

Also see "Our Favorite Vinaigrettes," page 112, and "Our Favorite Weeknight Pastas," page 130.

Essential Flavors

Roasted-Garlic Oil

3 heads garlic
2 teaspoons canola oil or safflower oil
1 cup extra-virgin olive oil, or ½ cup olive oil and ½ cup
canola oil or safflower oil

1. Preheat the oven to 400°F.

2. Lightly coat the garlic heads with 1 of the teaspoons of canola oil. Roast for 40 minutes. Remove from the oven and set aside until cool enough to handle.

3. With a serrated knife, split the garlic heads in half horizontally and squeeze the roasted garlic paste into a saucepan. Cover with the olive oil and warm gently for 5 minutes. Pour into a very clean jar, let cool, cover, and let steep in the refrigerator for 48 hours.

4. Line a funnel with a paper coffee filter and use a pastry brush to paint the filter with the remaining teaspoon of canola oil. Pour the Roasted-Garlic Oil into the filter and let it drip through the funnel into another very clean jar or bottle (this may take some time). Cover or cork tightly and label with the date. Store refrigerated.

MAKES ABOUT 1 CUP.

Applications

Neo-Classic Caesar Salad
Capellini with Roasted-Garlic Oil, Eggplant, Roasted
Peppers, and Arugula

Poached Sausages and Potatoes with Heavenly Vinaigrette

Flank Steak Marinated in Plum Vinegar (Variation)

Roasted-Garlic String Beans

"Miracle" Cherry Tomatoes (Variation)

Baked Tomatoes with Cornbread Stuffing and Cumin Oil (Variation)

Also see "Our Favorite Weeknight Pastas," page 130.

CHAPTER TWO

Flavored Vinegars

O nce upon a time, about ten thousand years ago, somebody let a barrel of wine go bad, and vinegar was born. Vinegar, which in French is *vinaigre* (*vin* means "wine" and *aigre* means "sour"), is acidic, and its tartness balances perfectly against oil, which is why vinaigrette is such a perfect sauce. But that acidity also makes vinegar an ideal medium to flavor with herbs and fruits. Not only does the herb or fruit *flavor* the vinegar, but the acid in the vinegar also *preserves* the herb or fruit, allowing us to leave vinegars steeping for a much longer time than oils. Most of our vinegars are steeped with herbs, fruits, or spices for ten days to two weeks, then strained out. These flavored vinegars have a long shelf life—from six months to a year—as long as they're stored in a cool, dry place.

Flavoring a bottle of vinegar with just a branch or two of herbs has become more and more popular in recent years, and of course this makes a beautiful gift, especially if presented in an attractive bottle. With this type of flavored vinegar, one usually leaves the herb in the bottle as long as the vinegar is being used. The difference between that method

Making Your Own Vinegar

Hold it! Don't pour out the end of that bottle of red wine that's turning a little sour. Why not start making your own vinegar with it? Once you do, you'll be so delighted with the deep, soft flavors that you'll be upset you never thought of doing this before.

To start, you'll need a mother. No, not *that* kind of mother: this one is a little blob of bacteria, a murky, slimy mass that sits in the vinegar, helping the wine that you'll be adding to ferment into vinegar—a bit like a sourdough starter.

If you have a friend who's making vinegar at home, he or she can simply cut a little piece off the mother to give you. Otherwise, you can purchase a bottle of mother of vinegar or unpasteurized vinegar.* In either case, fill a large glass container, preferably with a wide mouth, with leftover red wine, not more than halfway (much less is fine, too). Cover it with one layer of cheesecloth secured with a

*Available by mail order through, among others, Beer and Wine Hobby, (800) 523-5423; Cantinetta Tra Vigne, (707) 963-8888; and Beer and Wine Crafts, (619) 447-9191.

and ours is that we use a higher proportion of flavoring to imbue the vinegar with the *essence* of the flavoring. When you smell a bottle of Opal Basil Vinegar, for instance, you'll really smell opal basil—the vinegar aromas come out behind it. As a result, the jar in which the herbs are steeping in the vinegar is often rather crowded with herbs or fruit. After the initial steeping period, the flavoring will be strained out, so the flavoring process will be arrested at this point. The advantage to straining all the flavorings out is that one can control the intensity of the flavor. Our flavored vinegars are fairly uniform, and if we call for a certain amount in a recipe, you can be sure that it'll be about the same intensity when you reproduce the recipe in your kitchen.

The flavored-vinegar recipes included in this chapter each call for a particular type of vinegar—red wine vinegar, white wine (or champagne) vinegar, rice wine vinegar—or a combination of vinegars. If you have brands of these vinegars that you've already come to love, go ahead and use those. Otherwise, consider the relative acidity of the vinegars from which you're choosing—you'll find it right on the label in the form of a percentage. Most domestic vinegars are about 5 percent acidity; some imported ones are stronger, up to 8½ percent. A higher acidity can make some vinegars more flavorful, but it can also make inferior vinegars rather harsh. And price is not always a reliable indicator as to the quality of vinegar. In a blind tasting organized by *Cook's Illustrated* magazine, the number-one vinegar selected by the panel was Heinz Gourmet Fine Wine Vinegar, which at the time of the survey cost about $1.69 for twelve ounces; the number-six vinegar was a $20 vinegar from Italy! Rice wine vinegar is always fairly low in acid, usually a little over 4 percent, which is the minimum acidity for commercial vinegars.

Equipment and General Instructions:

Jars and bottles: To make the vinegars, you'll need some very large (32-ounce) mason or other jars for the initial steeping (the part of the process when you cram all the herbs or fruit in with the vinegar). To store the final product, jars are fine, though we prefer large glass bottles; you'll need appropriately sized corks to fit them snugly. Use glass jars or bottles only, as metal might react with the vinegar, causing off-flavors to develop. You may want to sterilize them before both steps (steeping and storing); in any case, they should be as clean as possible to prevent unwanted bacterial growth.

Funnel and cheesecloth: These will help you in straining the herbs or fruit out of the vinegar. These, too, should be as clean as possible.

The process: Our flavored vinegars are made by heating a commercial vinegar or combination of vinegars in a saucepan to between 100°F. and 110°F., which is warm but not hot to the touch. (Heating them more than that may alter the flavor of the vinegar.) We pour them over the flavoring ingredients in a mason jar, let them cool completely, cover them tightly with a very clean lid, and store them in a cool, dark place. After they've steeped for the appropriate length of time, we strain out the flavorings through a cheesecloth-lined funnel into a very clean glass bottle, cork it tightly, and store it out of the light. There is no need to refrigerate the vinegars.

rubber band, give it a few swirls to let a bunch of oxygen in, and let it sit overnight. Then add either the mother or all of the unpasteurized vinegar, and leave the container in a dark, warm (72°F. to 90°F.) place. If you have some more leftover red wine at any point, go ahead and add it, but make sure not to fill the container more than two-thirds full, since it needs a lot of oxygen to ferment. After two weeks to a month, or perhaps a little longer, you'll see something slimy on top—that's the mother. Pour off a bottle or two from the container, cork it tightly, and voilà! There's your homemade vinegar. Now just continue adding leftover wine (white is okay at this point, too) to the large container and pouring it off every so often. If you want the end-all of vinegars, take a bottle or two of your homemade stuff and age it for a few months. Your simplest vinaigrettes—or those made with flavored oils—will be major events!

Sage Vinegar

½ ounce fresh sage (½ cup chopped leaves)
2 cups white wine vinegar

1. Rinse and chop the sage and put it in a very clean mason jar. Warm the vinegar until it is warm to the touch but not hot and pour it over the herbs. Let cool, cover, and label with the date. Let stand in a cool, dark place for 2 weeks.

2. Strain through a cheesecloth-lined funnel into a very clean bottle and cover or cork tightly. Store in a cool, dark place.

MAKES ABOUT 2 CUPS.

Applications

Leeks with Sage Vinaigrette
Pork Chops Deglazed with Sage Vinegar and Currants
Poached Sausages and Potatoes with Heavenly Vinaigrette

Drizzle on Risotto Cakes, page 151.

Also see "Our Favorite Vinaigrettes," page 112.

Plum Vinegar

5 or 6 plums
1 cup cider vinegar
1 cup red wine vinegar
2 tablespoons balsamic vinegar

1. To peel plums easily, submerge them in boiling water for 45 seconds, then plunge them into ice water. Slip off the skins, cut the plums in half, remove the pits, and then slice. This should yield about 2 cups of sliced plums.

2. Combine the vinegars in a small saucepan and heat until warm to the touch but not hot. Place the peeled fruit in a very large, very clean mason jar and pour the vinegar over it. When cool, cover, label with the date, and store in a cool, dark place for 10 to 12 days.

3. Strain through a cheesecloth-lined funnel into a very clean bottle, pressing on the solids with the back of a wooden spoon; cover or cork tightly. Store in a cool, dark place.

MAKES ABOUT 1¾ CUPS.

Applications

Roast Chicken with Plum Vinegar Pan Sauce
Magret (Duck Breast) with Blackberry Vinegar Sauce
Flank Steak Marinated in Plum Vinegar
Braised Red Cabbage with Blackberry Vinegar (Variation)

Lemon Grass–Star Anise Vinegar

Fresh lemon grass may be found in many Asian groceries. Look for stalks that aren't shriveled-looking, though it's fine if they have some brown near the top, as you'll peel that part off. Look for star anise in the spice section of Asian or Latin American groceries if you don't see it at your supermarket.

10 stalks fresh lemon grass (about ½ pound)
16 star anise (or about 4 tablespoons if broken up)
2⅔ cups rice wine vinegar

1. Remove the dried outer leaves from the lemon grass and wash the tender stalks. Using a mallet, rolling pin, or other heavy object, bruise the lemon grass. Cut into ¼-inch pieces.

2. Place the lemon grass, star anise, and vinegar in a small saucepan and heat to just below a simmer. Let cool, pour into a very clean jar, cover, label with the date, and let steep in a cool, dark place for 12 to 14 days.

3. Strain through a cheesecloth-lined funnel into a very clean bottle; cover or cork tightly and store in a cool, dark place.

MAKES ABOUT 2½ CUPS.

Applications

Seared Scallops with Lemon Grass–Star Anise Vinegar
Black & White Sesame Salmon

Also see "Our Favorite Vinaigrettes," page 112.

Pink Tarragon Vinegar

Tarragon vinegar is, of course, widely available in stores, but should you have the urge to make a very tarragon-y version of your own, this is a nice way to do it.

2 bundles fresh tarragon, about 1 ounce each
2 cups white wine vinegar
1 cup red wine vinegar

1. Rinse the tarragon and discard any blackened leaves. Put all the tarragon into a large, very clean jar. Combine the two vinegars in a saucepan and heat until warm to the touch but not hot. Pour the vinegar over the herbs and swirl it around to make sure the herbs are covered. Let cool, cover, label with the date, and let stand in a cool, dark place for 10 to 12 days.

2. Strain through a cheesecloth-lined funnel into a very clean jar or bottle; cover or cork tightly. Store in a cool, dark place.

MAKES ABOUT 3 CUPS.

Applications

Poached Sausages and Potatoes with Heavenly Vinaigrette
Roast Asparagus with Pink Tarragon Vinegar
Roast Chicken with Plum Vinegar Pan Sauce (Variation)

Drizzle on Risotto Cakes, page 151.

Also see "Our Favorite Vinaigrettes," page 112.

Opal Basil Vinegar

This purple member of the basil family imparts a deep, bright, almost figgy flavor and a divine amethyst color to this vinegar.

1 bundle fresh opal (purple) basil leaves (about 1 ounce)
2 cups white wine vinegar

1. Rinse the basil and discard any blackened leaves. Put all the basil into a very clean jar. Heat the vinegar until warm to the touch but not hot, pour it over the herbs, and swirl it around to make sure the herbs are covered. Let cool, cover, label with the date, and let stand in a cool, dark place for 10 to 14 days.

2. Strain through a cheesecloth-lined funnel into a very clean jar or bottle; cover or cork tightly. Keep in a cool, dark place.

MAKES ABOUT 2 CUPS.

Applications

Poached Sausages and Potatoes with Heavenly Vinaigrette

Pork Medallions on a Bed of Parsnip Purée with Opal Basil Vinegar Sauce

Couscous with Currants, Scallions, and Opal Basil Vinaigrette

Roast Chicken with Plum Vinegar Pan Sauce (Variation)

Also see "Our Favorite Vinaigrettes," page 112.

Bouquet de Provence
Red Wine Vinegar

The herbs and garlic of Provence combine here to make a lovely all-purpose red wine vinegar. Since many herbs come in 1-ounce packages, you may want to double or even quadruple the recipe—lay down the extra bottles in a cool, dark place to age and they'll get even better. And, of course, small bottles of this make wonderful gifts. If you happen to make your own vinegar, this is a terrific way to make it even more heavenly (but skip the heating part in step 2—you don't want to alter what you've gone to the trouble to make delicious already).

¼ **ounce fresh thyme**
¼ **ounce fresh marjoram or fresh oregano**
¼ **ounce fresh rosemary (4 or 5 sprigs)**
12 to 14 fresh sage leaves
2 garlic cloves, smashed with the side of a knife and peeled
2 bay leaves
3 cups red wine vinegar

1. Rinse the thyme, marjoram, rosemary, and sage and pat them dry. Bruise the thyme and rosemary with a rolling pin, mallet, or other heavy object. Place them in a large, very clean jar along with the marjoram, sage, garlic, and bay leaves.

2. Heat the vinegar in a saucepan until it is warm to the touch but not hot and pour it over the herbs. Let cool, seal the jar, label with the date, and place in a cool, dark place for 2 to 3 weeks.

3. Strain through a funnel lined with several layers of cheese-cloth into a very clean bottle; close tightly with a cork. Store in a cool, dark place.

MAKES ABOUT 2¾ CUPS.

Applications

Neo-Classic Caesar Salad
Bistro Salad
Poached Sausages and Potatoes with Heavenly Vinaigrette
Roast Leg of Lamb with Roasted-Garlic Essence

Also see "Our Favorite Vinaigrettes," page 112.

Mint Vinegar

1 large bunch fresh mint
1 cup white wine vinegar
1 cup red wine vinegar

1. Wash the mint, pat it dry, and strip the leaves off the larger stems. Discard any leaves that are turning black. Place the green leaves in a very clean jar.

2. Combine the vinegars in a saucepan, heat until warm to the touch but not hot, and pour them over the mint. Let cool, cover, label with the date, and let steep in a cool, dark place for 4 days.

3. Strain through a cheesecloth-lined sieve into a very clean bottle, pressing on the mint with the back of a wooden spoon; cover or cork tightly. Store in a cool, dark place.

MAKES JUST UNDER 2 CUPS.

Applications

Minted Beet Salad
Lamb Chops with Mint Vinegar

Blackberry Vinegar

Introducing the more interesting, more sophisticated cousin of raspberry vinegar! This doesn't have the cloying sweetness of raspberry vinegar, but it does have a deeply berry flavor.

12 ounces fresh blackberries
2 cups white wine vinegar or champagne vinegar

1. Gently rinse the fruit and place it in a very large, very clean mason jar. Heat the vinegar in a saucepan until warm to the touch but not hot and pour over the fruit. Let cool completely, then cover tightly, label with the date, and store in a cool, dark place for 10 to 12 days.

2. Strain through a cheesecloth-lined funnel into a very clean bottle, pressing on the solids with the back of a wooden spoon; cover or cork tightly. Store in a cool, dark place.

MAKES ABOUT 1¾ CUPS.

Applications

Magret (Duck Breast) with Blackberry Vinegar Sauce
Braised Red Cabbage with Blackberry Vinegar
Roast Chicken with Plum Vinegar Pan Sauce (Variation)
Pork Medallions on a Bed of Parsnip Purée with Opal Basil
   Vinegar Sauce (Variation)

CHAPTER THREE

Essences and Elixirs

The third and fourth elements in our Pantry of Potential are essences and elixirs, our new allies in the kitchen. We use them as shortcuts to flavor in soups, pastas, and salads; with a few of these stashed in the refrigerator or freezer, we're no longer daunted by the prospect of turning out a sauce for an important roast or a fancy dessert. Technically, we think of essences and elixirs as the opposite of each other: Essences are thick concentrations, which we roast or cook to remove the water and intensify the flavors. Elixirs, on the other hand, are water- or alcohol-based liquids in which we steep some potent ingredient. The steeping takes as little as eight minutes or as long as seven days.

Essences: Each is slightly different, and as you might expect, each requires different cooking times and methods. Some are thick enough to fortify a soup, others thin enough to be worked into a vinaigrette. In certain essences, ingredients—such as garlic or red peppers—change their character almost completely. Our most intense essence, Roasted-Beet Essence, is so deep and silky it might even convert a beet-o-phobic or two. Most essences are savory; our single sweet essence, simmered on top of the stove, captures the summer flavor of sweet, plump figs.

Once an essence has been made and cooled, we stash it away in a clean jar, labeled with the date and contents. All of the essences keep for at least a week in the refrigerator. We have also had a great deal of success with freezing essences in resealable freezer bags.

Elixirs: To some, the word "elixir" means a magic potion bestowing eternal life; to others, it signifies a cure-all or a substance that transmutes dross into gold. The elixirs in *Essential Flavors* perform all of these tricks—our favorite kind of kitchen alchemy. They give new life to ingredients, even those that might otherwise have been tossed out, and they transform even the tiredest old dishes into something new and delicious.

Some are water-based, such as Peppermint Elixir—a doubly strong brew of dried peppermint leaves and water—and Sun-Dried Tomato Elixir, the result of a happy accident that occurs when we reconstitute sun-dried tomatoes.

Other elixirs are alcohol-based. One day in May, after the Kentucky Derby, we combined mint and bourbon and left it to steep. The tipsy result was Mint Julep Elixir—it's the secret ingredient in a mighty fine bread pudding. We were so pleased with the Mint Julep Elixir that we scraped the flavorful dark seeds out of a couple of vanilla beans and put them in a jar with some golden rum. The resulting elixir is very sophisticated, very rummy, very vanilla.

Some of the elixirs need to be simmered for a while to accelerate the marriage of ingredients. We simmer a bottle or two of red wine with a basic "mirepoix" (diced celery, carrots, and onions) to achieve that deep wininess that we associate with long-cooking daubes and stews.

Ruby port gets a kick from freshly ground black pepper and an earthy background note from fresh sage when we cook them together for a mere twenty minutes. We put the resulting elixir in a bottle and bring it out when we need a quick dessert sauce or even a deglazing sauce for a roast duck.

All the elixirs should be kept in clean, labeled bottles. Some need refrigeration; others do not.

This collection of essences and elixirs is just the beginning. Once you begin to play around with the concept, dozens of ideas will occur to you. Soon you, too, will be creating your own Pantry of Potential.

Roasted-Tomato Essence

A great way to capture the essential flavor of plum tomatoes and preserve it in big batches. The long, slow roasting concentrates even the meager taste of "winter" tomatoes, giving them a slightly sweet, caramelized flavor that adds character to soups, stews, and pasta sauces. This is a lovely substitute for canned tomato paste, which has always tasted slightly metallic to us. Consider doubling the recipe at summer's end, when plum tomatoes are plentiful and cheap, and freezing the essence in resealable freezer bags.

3 pounds fresh plum tomatoes (do not use canned)
1 teaspoon olive oil
½ teaspoon salt
½ teaspoon freshly ground black pepper

1. Preheat the oven to 250°F.

2. Wash the tomatoes and split them lengthwise. Oil a large shallow baking pan (13 inches x 17 inches) and sprinkle the salt over its surface. Place the tomatoes, cut side down, on the pan. Bake in the oven for 2 to 2½ hours, or until the tomatoes are deflated, crinkled-looking, and slightly browned.

3. Put all the tomatoes in a food processor, add the pepper, and process briefly. The sauce should be thick and slightly chunky. Store refrigerated.

MAKES ABOUT 1½ CUPS.

Variation:

Add a teaspoon of your choice of infused oils as the essence
is processed.

Applications

Spicy Winter Soup with Roasted-Tomato Essence

Chicken Oven-Braised in Roasted-Tomato Essence with
    Cinnamon, Bay Leaf, and Onions

*Spread lavishly on sandwiches in place of anemic winter
tomatoes.*

*Also see "Our Favorite Vinaigrettes," page 112, and "Our
Favorite Weeknight Pastas," page 130.*

Caramelized-Shallot Essence

We couldn't live without this member of the pantry, which has a sweet, rich flavor all its own. It would be impossible to list all its applications—we swirl a teaspoon of this into dozens of dishes. It acts as an instant flavor booster in simple broths, transforms ordinary pan gravies into luxurious sauces, and elevates workaday pastas into savory supper fare.

3 tablespoons olive oil
16 medium shallots (about 1 pound), thinly sliced

1. Gently heat the olive oil in a heavy-bottomed sauté pan. Add the shallots and cook them over very low heat, stirring occasionally, making sure they don't brown, until they're caramelized (sweet, soft, and translucent caramel color), 45 minutes to 1 hour and 20 minutes.

2. Purée in a food processor or blender until smooth. Store refrigerated in a very clean jar, tightly covered.

MAKES ABOUT ⅔ CUP.

Applications

Roast Chicken with Plum Vinegar Pan Sauce (Variation)

Also see "Our Favorite Weeknight Pastas," page 130.

Make canapés with toast rounds spread with this essence and topped with niçoise olives or anchovies.

Spread on a roast beef sandwich.

Drop a few dollops on top of a homemade pizza before baking.

Roasted Red Pepper Essence

3 medium red bell peppers

1. Preheat the broiler. To roast the peppers, cut them in half vertically, lay them skin side up on a broiler tray, and place them under the broiler until the skins are completely charred. Put them in a paper bag and roll the bag shut. Set aside for 10 to 15 minutes to let the skins loosen.

2. Using a small paring knife, remove the seeds and pull away the inner membranes. Remove the blackened skin. Do not rinse, as this will dilute the flavor.

3. Place the peppers in the bowl of a food processor or blender and purée until smooth.

MAKES ¾ CUP TO 1 CUP.

Applications

Fennel Soup with Roasted Red Pepper Essence

Grilled Chicken Breasts with Roasted Red Pepper–Chive–Lime Sauce

Also see "Our Favorite Weeknight Pastas," page 130.

Use as a spread for sandwiches. (Try fresh mozzarella, tomato, and arugula on a French roll with Roasted Red Pepper Essence spread on one side of the bread, and Rosemary Oil or Basil Oil mixed with red wine vinegar drizzled on the other side—irresistible!)

Roasted-Garlic Essence

If you roast several heads of garlic at once, you'll have enough of this indispensable essence to get you through the week. Store it in a glass bowl or container rather than in plastic.

6 heads garlic
1 teaspoon olive oil

1. Preheat the oven to 400°F.

2. Place the garlic heads in a pan and lightly rub them with the oil. Roast for 40 minutes. Remove from the oven and let stand until cool enough to handle.

3. Using a serrated knife, cut the garlic in half horizontally. Squeeze the paste out into a clean bowl. Keep refrigerated and well covered in a glass container.

MAKES 1 TO 1⅓ CUPS, DEPENDING ON THE SIZE OF THE GARLIC HEADS.

Applications

Roast Leg of Lamb with Roasted-Garlic Essence
Roast Chicken with Plum Vinegar Pan Sauce (Variation)

Stir into pasta sauce (or a prepared spaghetti sauce).

Spread on baguettes (as the French do by squeezing roasted garlic cloves).

Roasted-Beet Essence

1 pound beets, weighed without the greens (about 5 or 6 medium beets)

1. Preheat the oven to 400°F.

2. Trim the beets but do not peel them. Wrap each beet individually in aluminum foil and put them in the oven. Roast for 1 hour. (Check for doneness by sticking a fork into one of them through the foil—it should be tender.) Unwrap foil and set beets aside until cool enough to handle.

3. Peel the beets—the jackets should come off very easily with the help of a small paring knife. Cut them into quarters and juice in a juicer. Since the juice will be thick, be sure to check for any that has collected in front of the pouring spout of the juicer. (NOTE: If you don't have a juicer, process in the bowl of a food processor until very smooth, then force through a sieve into a bowl.)

MAKES ABOUT 1 CUP.

Applications

Chilled Cucumber Soup with Roasted-Beet Essence
Fennel Salad with Roasted-Beet Essence and Orange Zest

Fig Essence

This essence makes use of those lovely small black mission figs that appear as the final curtain call of summer's bountiful performance. We buy them by the pint when we can, and there are always some smashed or slightly moldy figs on the bottom. With a quick rinse, even these bottom figs are fine for this recipe.

1 pound fresh small black mission figs
2 tablespoons dry white wine
2 tablespoons fresh lemon juice
1 teaspoon vanilla extract or Vanilla-Rum Elixir (page 80)
1 tablespoon sugar
two 1-inch-long strips of lemon zest

1. Wash the figs and chop them coarsely. Combine all ingredients in a saucepan and cook, covered, over medium heat for 10 to 15 minutes, stirring every 4 to 5 minutes.

2. Pour the contents of the saucepan into a food mill or sieve placed over a large bowl. Force the fig essence through the food mill or sieve until all that remains behind are the fig skins, lemon zest, and a bit of fig pulp, which you can discard. The Fig Essence in the bowl should be almost jam-like in consistency. Transfer to a clean container and refrigerate for later use or use immediately.

MAKES ABOUT 1 CUP.

Applications

Cornish Game Hens with Fig Essence and Cognac
Lindsay Torte, or Fig Essence and Pistachio Tart
Fig Essence Ice Cream

Use as a topping for waffles.

Smear on a slice of country bread for an Aegean breakfast.

Leek Elixir

You'll never throw away leek tops again! Sometimes we make Leeks Vinaigrette just so we can use the tops for Leek Elixir. It's so good, we've been tempted to drink it plain.

green parts of 6 to 8 leeks
1 cup dry white wine
3 tablespoons fresh thyme or 1½ tablespoons dried
2 tablespoons black peppercorns
1 teaspoon salt

1. Wash the leek tops, rinsing them thoroughly in at least three or four changes of water to make sure you get rid of all the grit that tends to be lodged between the leaves. Chop them into 1-inch strips. You should have about 8 cups, packed.

2. Combine all ingredients with 6 cups water in a large kettle or stockpot. Bring the water to a boil, reduce the heat, and simmer, partially covered, for 25 minutes. Remove from the heat and let stand 10 minutes.

3. Pour the Leek Elixir through a strainer into a very clean container and let cool. Cover and store refrigerated. Leek Elixir may also be frozen.

MAKES ABOUT 6 CUPS.

Applications

Saffron-Infused Broth with Shrimp and Scallop Ravioli
Orecchiette in Leek Elixir with Spinach

Risotto with Leek Elixir, Sun-Dried Tomatoes, and Parsley

Chicken Breasts with Rosemary-Leek Coulis

Chicken with Leek Elixir and Shallots

Wild and Basmati Rice with Leek Elixir

Use in place of chicken broth in just about anything—great for vegetarians!

Porcini Elixir

They're thinking of making it a crime to throw away the liquid left over from reconstituting dried porcini mushrooms—it's packed with deep, earthy flavor.

2 ounces dried porcini mushrooms (cèpes)
2 cups boiling water
⅛ teaspoon salt

1. Place the mushrooms in a bowl and pour the boiling water over them. Let soak 30 minutes.

2. Strain the elixir through a cheesecloth-lined strainer into a small saucepan, reserving the reconstituted mushrooms for another use.* Bring the elixir to a boil, reduce the heat, add the salt, and simmer for 10 minutes. To store, let cool, pour into a very clean jar, cover, and keep refrigerated.

MAKES 1¼ CUPS.

Applications

Roast Portobello Mushrooms with Porcini Elixir
Penne with Fresh and Wild Mushrooms and Rosemary Oil
Risotto with Roast Asparagus and Porcini Elixir
Veal Stew with Porcini Elixir and Kale
String Bean Purée with Porcini Elixir

Add to Bolognese sauce for pasta.

Such as Wild Mushroom Agnolotti with Thyme Oil (page 137) or Penne with Fresh and Wild Mushrooms and Rosemary Oil (page 144).

Essential Flavors

Red Wine Elixir

Slow reduction of red wine results in a versatile elixir with a deep yet mellow flavor that truly captures the essence of wine. Besides the applications you'll find in this book, use it to deglaze the pan for roasted or sautéed lamb, beef, chicken, or even salmon, or to perk up any kind of sauce or dish in which you'd normally be tempted to splash in some wine.

When selecting the wine, choose something drinkable yet inexpensive. Bordeaux works terrifically well, but so do California pinot noirs. More assertive wines, such as California or Chilean cabernets, will produce a stronger elixir that stands up to beef and lamb but may overpower chicken and fish.

While this elixir can be made in less than an hour by turning up the flame, the most flavorful results are yielded by long, slow simmering.

6 carrots, peeled and cut into small dice
6 stalks celery, cut into small dice
2 medium onions, cut into small dice
2 bottles inexpensive Bordeaux or other soft, drinkable red
  wine

1. Place the diced vegetables in a saucepan and pour the wine over them. Bring to a simmer and continue simmering, uncovered, over medium-low heat until reduced by two-thirds.

2. Pour the elixir through a strainer into a large measuring cup, pressing on the vegetables with the back of a wooden spoon to extract all the flavor. If you have more than 2 cups, return the elixir to the saucepan and reduce further.

If not using immediately, let cool, cover, and store refrigerated in a very clean jar or bottle.

MAKES 2 CUPS.

Applications

Hearts of Polenta with Wine-Dark Tomato Sauce
Roast Veal with Red Wine Elixir and Rosemary
Roast Chicken with Plum Vinegar Pan Sauce (Variation)

Add to prepared spaghetti sauce.

Use to deglaze the pan after roasting or sautéing.

Stir into canned lentil soup or minestrone.

Essential Flavors

Sun-Dried Tomato Elixir

This sunny elixir adds a mighty burst of flavor to sauces and salad dressings.

4 ounces sun-dried tomatoes (dry—not preserved in oil)
5⅓ cups boiling water

1. Place the sun-dried tomatoes in a bowl and pour the water over them. Let steep for 45 minutes.

2. Strain out the reconstituted tomato pieces and reserve them for another use.*

3. Place the Sun-Dried Tomato Elixir, which should measure about 4 cups, in a small saucepan, bring to a simmer, and continue simmering, uncovered, until the liquid is reduced by half.

MAKES ABOUT 2 CUPS.

Applications

Warmed Chèvre Salad with Sun-Dried Tomato Elixir
Risotto with Leek Elixir, Sun-Dried Tomatoes, and Parsley

Stir into pasta sauces.
Add to rice cooking water.

---

*Such as Pasta Paradiso (page 131), or Risotto with Leek Elixir, Sun-Dried Tomatoes, and Parsley (page 148).

Saffron Elixir

It takes 70,000 hand-picked crocus stamens to yield a pound of saffron, but fortunately you need to soak only a few of the lovely threads in a cup of hot water to create a golden elixir that adds exotic color and flavor to both broths and risottos.

½ teaspoon saffron threads, packed
1 cup boiling water

1. Pour the boiling water over the saffron threads in a small bowl. Let steep for 30 minutes. Strain, or leave the threads in for visual interest.

2. If not using immediately, pour into a very clean bottle or jar, close or cork tightly, and store refrigerated.

MAKES 1 CUP.

Applications

Saffron-Infused Broth with Shrimp and Scallop Ravioli
Seafood Risotto with Saffron Elixir

Substitute for part of the cooking water, for saffron rice.

Substitute for part of the water when preparing packaged couscous.

Port-Pepper-Sage Elixir

3 cups ruby port
1 bunch fresh sage, finely chopped (about 1 ounce)
3 to 4 grindings of black pepper

1. Combine the ingredients in a saucepan and bring to a boil.
   Reduce the heat and simmer, uncovered, 20 to 25 minutes,
   until the elixir has been reduced to 2 cups.

2. Strain into a very clean bottle, let cool, cover, and label.
   Store refrigerated.

MAKES 2 CUPS.

Applications

Roast Duck with Port-Pepper-Sage Sauce
Roast Pork with Port-Pepper-Sage Elixir
Peaches Poached in Port-Pepper-Sage Elixir

Reduce by half to use as sauce for vanilla ice cream.
Reduce by half, poke holes in angel food cake, and pour on top.

Peppermint Elixir

3 tablespoons dried peppermint (available in spice shops, or substitute 4 bags of peppermint herb tea)
2 cups boiling water

1. Place peppermint in a teapot or heatproof pitcher or bowl. Let the water stand for about 10 seconds (it should be just off boiling), then pour over the peppermint. Let steep 8 to 10 minutes. Do not let it steep too long or it will turn bitter.

2. Strain into a very clean jar, cover, and store in the refrigerator.

MAKES 1½ CUPS.

Applications

Chilled Minted Tomato Soup
Chocolate-Mint Pots de Crème
Mint-Infused Blackberry Ice

Plum Elixir

Sweet purple plums lend a glorious color and flavor to this elixir. Once poached, the plums you strain out can be served (with a little extra sugar or honey) as a snack.

½ cup dry white wine
⅓ cup Madeira or dry sherry
1 cup dark brown sugar, packed
one 2-inch piece fresh ginger root, peeled and thinly sliced
1 tablespoon black peppercorns
1 juice orange (all of its peel, peeled with a vegetable peeler, and all of its juice)
2 lemons (all of their peel, peeled with a vegetable peeler, and all of their juice)
3 star anise or 1 teaspoon fennel seeds
10 plums, rinsed

1. In a stockpot, combine all ingredients except the plums with 5 cups water. Bring to a boil, stirring occasionally. Reduce the heat and simmer for 10 minutes.

2. Cut an X at the bottom of each plum and add the plums to the poaching liquid. Poach 10 to 15 minutes, or until the skins start to loosen. With a slotted spoon, remove each plum, dunk it briefly in a bowl of ice water, and remove the skin. Reserve the plums for another use, if desired. Return the skins to the poaching liquid.

3. Continue simmering the poaching liquid for another 15 minutes. Strain the liquid and discard the solids. Return

the liquid to a saucepan and reduce until you have 2 cups
Plum Elixir.

MAKES 2 CUPS.

Applications

Mustard Pork Chops with Plum Elixir
Plum Elixir Ice Cream

Reduce by half to use as sauce for vanilla ice cream.

Mint Julep Elixir

Here's an elixir borrowed from the classic Virginia cocktail, based on the happy marriage of bourbon and mint.

2 cups fresh peppermint leaves, rinsed and patted dry
2 cups high-quality bourbon, such as Maker's Mark, Jack Daniel's, or Jim Beam

1. Remove any peppermint leaves that are turning black, as they will discolor the elixir. Using a mallet, rolling pin, or other heavy object, bruise the green leaves; place them in a very clean mason jar and pour the bourbon over them.

2. Cover the jar tightly and let steep for 24 hours, then strain through a cheesecloth-lined funnel into a very clean bottle or jar. Cover or cork tightly. Refrigeration is unnecessary.

MAKES 2 CUPS.

Applications

Mint Julep Bread Pudding
Mint Julep Ice Cream

Vanilla-Rum Elixir

2 cups golden rum, such as Mount Gay
4 vanilla beans

1. Pour the rum into a very clean jar. Split the vanilla beans lengthwise, scrape out the seeds in the center, and add the seeds to the rum. Cut the vanilla beans into 1-inch pieces and add to the rum. Let steep, covered, for 5 to 7 days.

2. Strain out the amount of elixir you need as you use it. Add replacement rum to the jar so that you always have some elixir on hand, steeping. You do not need to replace the vanilla beans each time, but you might want to add a new bean every other time you deplete your whole jar of elixir.

MAKES 2 CUPS.

Applications

Pear Fans Baked in Vanilla-Rum Elixir
Dried-Fruit Crumble with Vanilla-Rum Elixir and Coconut
Vanilla-Rum Elixir Tea Cake

Use instead of commercial vanilla extract in any dessert.

PART TWO

Essential Flavors on the Table

How to Use Infused Oils, Flavored Vinegars, Essences, and Elixirs to Create Memorable Meals

Now that you've brewed a tantalizing collection of infused oils and flavored vinegars, you're probably wondering how to cook with them. Maybe you cautiously roasted some tomatoes, or simmered a batch of Red Wine Elixir, and need something to make for dinner tonight. Possibly you threw yourself into the Pantry of Potential with abandon and want to know what on earth you're going to do with the Fig Essence, the Lemon Grass–Star Anise Vinegar, the Shallot Oil you've created.

The answers lie in the next section of *Essential Flavors*. We don't attempt to provide a comprehensive culinary encyclopedia of recipes here. Rather, we've tried to touch on a range of offerings, from simple family meals to fancy fare for dinner parties, from salads that are on the lean side of the scale to recipes for the cholesterolly unconcerned. Our intention is to give you an idea of how easy it is to incorporate these bright new ingredients into recipe concepts already familiar to you. At the same time, you will find a selection of fresh new ideas for those moments when you want to expand your culinary repertoire.

CHAPTER FOUR

Openers

Common menu-planning wisdom holds that the two most important courses in a meal are the appetizer and the dessert. The dessert sends people away from a luscious finale, letting them linger with good memories of the meal. The appetizer, on the other hand, both starts off the meal with a good first impression and sets the tone for what's to come.

The French call the first course the *entrée,* which confuses Americans visiting France. Literally, *entrée* means "entrance," as in the entrance to a meal. To us, starting off a meal with a little savory something is what civilization is all about. We call them "openers," for they open up the dining experience.

In this chapter you'll find a dozen or so lovely ways to begin a meal; but in Chapter Five you'll also find several salads that can be served as openers, and just about all the pastas and risottos in Chapter Six work as openers, too.

Roasted-Beet Essence

1 pound beets, weighed without the greens (about 5 or 6 medium beets)

1. Preheat oven to 400°F.

2. Trim the beets but do not peel them. Wrap each beet individually in aluminum foil and put them in the oven. Roast for 1 hour. (Check for doneness by sticking a fork into one of them through the foil—it should be tender.) Unwrap foil and set beets aside until cool enough to handle.

3. Peel the beets—the jackets should come off very easily with the help of a small paring knife. Cut them into quarters and juice in a juicer. Since the juice will be thick, be sure to check for any that has collected in front of the pouring spout of the juicer. (NOTE: If you don't have a juicer, process in the bowl of a food processor until very smooth, then force through a sieve into a bowl.)

Makes about 1 cup.

Chilled Cucumber Soup with Roasted-Beet Essence

Wonderfully refreshing for a summer evening, and gorgeous to boot—pale green, with vivid swirls of fuchsia.

5 cucumbers
3 tablespoons unsalted butter
⅔ cup chopped white onion
salt
freshly ground white pepper
3 cups homemade chicken stock (or 1½ cups canned plus 1½ cups water)
⅓ cup crème fraîche (page 254) or sour cream
⅓ cup plus 1 tablespoon Roasted-Beet Essence
1 tablespoon fennel leaves (the feathery tops) or fresh dill, for garnish

1. Peel the cucumbers and cut off the stem ends. Slice in half vertically, scoop out the seeds with a spoon, and discard. Chop the seeded cucumbers roughly.

2. In a large saucepan or stockpot, melt the butter, add the onion, and sauté until soft over low heat, 7 to 8 minutes. Add cucumbers, salt, and pepper, raise heat to medium, and sauté for 10 minutes, until cucumbers start to turn translucent. Add the chicken stock, bring to a boil, turn down heat to medium, and simmer for 5 minutes. Purée the soup until smooth in a food processor or blender and chill thoroughly.

3. After the soup is chilled, whisk in 2 tablespoons of the crème fraîche and adjust seasoning. To serve, ladle a por-

tion of soup into a chilled soup plate and then take 1 tablespoon of Roasted-Beet Essence and swirl it into a decorative circle in the middle of the cucumber soup. Top with 1 teaspoon of crème fraîche and sprinkle a few pretty fennel or dill leaves on top.

SERVES 6.

Chilled Minted Tomato Soup

Peppermint Elixir

3 tablespoons dried peppermint (available in spice shops, or substitute 4 bags of peppermint herb tea)
2 cups boiling water

1. Place peppermint in a teapot or heatproof pitcher or bowl. Let water stand for about 10 seconds (it should be just off boiling), then pour over the peppermint. Let steep 8 to 10 minutes. Do not let it steep too long or it will turn bitter.

2. Strain into a very clean jar, cover, and store in the refrigerator.

Makes 1½ cups.

We make this on summer mornings so that it will be chilled and ready to refresh us after a sun-filled day at the beach.

2½ pounds very ripe summer tomatoes
1 tablespoon vegetable oil or canola oil
1 onion, chopped
1 carrot, peeled and sliced thin
1 cup homemade chicken stock (or ⅔ cup canned plus
    ⅓ cup water)
½ cup Peppermint Elixir
2 bay leaves
salt
freshly ground white pepper
1 teaspoon Mint Oil (optional)
sprigs of mint, for garnish

1. Peel and seed tomatoes and chop roughly. (Plunge tomatoes into boiling water for 10 seconds, then submerge in ice water. Skins will slip off easily.) Heat vegetable oil in a large saucepan or stockpot, add onions and carrots, and cook on medium-low heat until carrots are tender, about 10 minutes. Do not let onions brown. Add tomatoes, stock, Peppermint Elixir, bay leaves, salt, and pepper, bring to a simmer, and continue simmering for 10 minutes.

2. Remove bay leaves and purée soup in a food processor or blender until smooth. Adjust seasonings. Force through a sieve (do not omit this step). Whisk in Mint Oil, if desired, and chill. Serve chilled, garnished with sprigs of fresh mint.

SERVES 4.

Saffron-Infused Broth with Shrimp and Scallop Ravioli

This is a lovely soup for a special occasion, and making the ravioli using wonton wrappers is a breeze. The broth is simplicity itself, yet its gorgeous perfume will delight your guests.

For the ravioli:
12 medium shrimp (about ¼ pound)
salt
freshly ground white pepper
12 plump bay scallops, or 4 or 5 sea scallops, sliced
horizontally into ⅓-inch slices (about ¼ pound)
one 12-ounce package wonton skins (wrappers), defrosted
if frozen
1 egg, beaten

For the broth:
¾ cup Saffron Elixir, reserving threads for garnish
6 cups homemade chicken stock (or 2½ cups canned
chicken broth plus 1½ cups water plus 2 cups Leek
Elixir)
salt
freshly ground white pepper

1. To make the ravioli, peel and devein the shrimp and sprinkle with salt and pepper. Sprinkle the scallops with salt and pepper as well. Lay a wonton skin on your workboard, place a scallop in the center, and curve a shrimp around it. Using a pastry brush, paint some beaten egg in a diamond shape around the scallop and shrimp, and lay another wonton square over it, but rotated 45 degrees from the bottom one, so the two wonton skins form an

Saffron Elixir

½ teaspoon saffron threads, packed
1 cup boiling water

1. Pour the boiling water over the saffron threads in a small bowl. Let steep for 30 minutes. Strain, or leave threads in for visual interest.

2. If not using immediately, pour into a very clean bottle or jar, close or cork tightly, and store refrigerated.

Makes 1 cup.

eight-pointed star. Press dough together around the sea-food, pushing any air bubbles out to the sides. Seal completely and place on a tray lined with parchment or wax paper. Continue until you have 12 ravioli, separating each layer with paper. Cover and refrigerate until ready for use. (NOTE: May be prepared to this point several hours ahead of time.)

2. To make the broth, combine the Saffron Elixir and chicken stock in a large, wide kettle and bring to a simmer. Adjust seasoning and remove from heat if not serving immediately. When ready to serve, bring broth to a simmer again, and use a slotted spoon to lower the ravioli into the simmering broth. Let them cook gently for 4 to 5 minutes, until the shrimp become visibly pink through the pasta. Gently remove them with a slotted spoon, placing two in each soup plate. Ladle a portion of the broth over the ravioli and scatter a few saffron threads on top.

SERVES 6.

Sweet Pea Soup Kissed with Lemon

If you're the sneaky type, you can let your guests think you shelled 8,000 peas for this lush soup, which positively sings with the essence of fresh peas. The trick? They're frozen!

½ stick unsalted butter
1 head Boston lettuce, rinsed and cut into shreds
6 cups tiny frozen peas (2 pounds), defrosted
1 teaspoon sugar
salt
freshly ground pepper
2 tablespoons Lemon-Herb Oil

1. Melt butter in a large kettle or stockpot; add lettuce and cook over low heat for 5 minutes. Add peas, stir to combine, and cook, uncovered, stirring occasionally, for 15 minutes. Add 3 cups water, bring to a simmer, and continue to simmer, uncovered, for 40 minutes.

2. Purée the soup until smooth in a food processor or blender (this will require several batches). Return the soup to the kettle, add the sugar, salt, and pepper, and heat through. Whisk in Lemon-Herb Oil and serve in warmed soup plates.

SERVES 4 TO 6.

Lemon-Herb Oil

1 lemon
1 ounce fresh thyme
1 cup plus 1 teaspoon canola oil or safflower oil

1. With a vegetable peeler, peel the yellow zest from the lemon, making sure to leave the white pith on the fruit. Wash the thyme, then break it up and "bruise" it using a mallet, rolling pin, or other heavy object. Put the thyme in a saucepan with the lemon zest and the cup of oil. Warm gently over low heat for 5 minutes. Pour into a very clean jar, let cool, cover, and let steep in the refrigerator for 24 to 48 hours.

2. Line a funnel with a paper coffee filter and use a pastry brush to paint the filter with the remaining teaspoon of oil. Pour the Lemon-Herb Oil into the filter and let it drip through the funnel into another very clean jar or bottle (this may take some time). Cover or cork tightly and label with the date. Store refrigerated.

Makes about 1 cup.

3 medium red bell peppers

1. Preheat the broiler. To roast the peppers, cut them in half vertically, lay them skin side up on a broiler tray, and place them under the broiler until the skins are completely charred. Put them in a paper bag and roll the bag shut. Set aside for 10 to 15 minutes to let the skins loosen.

2. Using a small paring knife, remove the seeds and pull away the inner membranes. Remove the blackened skin. Do not rinse, as this will dilute the flavor.

3. Place the peppers in the bowl of a food processor or blender and purée until smooth.

Makes ¾ cup to I cup.

Fennel Soup with Roasted Red Pepper Essence

Silky Roasted Red Pepper Essence, swirled into a tomato-y fennel soup—close your eyes and you could be in the Tuscan hilltown of Siena.

2 tablespoons fennel seeds
3 tablespoons olive oil
2 onions, finely chopped
2 fennel bulbs, trimmed, cored, and sliced into thin arcs and strips (save some of the feathery green tops for garnish)
3 plum tomatoes (canned), seeded and diced
1 bay leaf
3½ cups homemade chicken stock, or 2½ cups canned plus 1 cup water
1 cup dry white wine
salt
freshly ground pepper
½ cup Roasted Red Pepper Essence
½ cup coarsely grated Parmesan cheese (optional)

1. Toast the fennel seeds in a dry sauté pan until they begin to turn color and announce their aroma.

2. Gently heat the olive oil in a large stockpot and add the chopped onions. Cook over medium heat for 10 minutes, add the fennel seeds, and cook for another 5 minutes, or until the onions are soft. Add the fennel slices, tomatoes, bay leaf, chicken stock, wine, and 2 cups water. Bring to a boil, reduce heat to a bare simmer, and cook, uncovered, for 30 minutes.

3. Remove from heat and season to taste with salt and pepper. Remove the bay leaf. Let the soup stand for 10 to 15 minutes. Reheat before serving.

4. To serve, ladle the soup into individual soup bowls and put a healthy tablespoon of the Roasted Red Pepper Essence in the center of each bowl. Garnish with the feathery fennel tops and, if desired, grated Parmesan cheese.

SERVES 6.

Roasted-Tomato Essence

3 pounds fresh plum tomatoes (do not use canned)
1 teaspoon olive oil
½ teaspoon salt
½ teaspoon freshly ground black pepper

1. Preheat the oven to 250°F.

2. Wash the tomatoes and split them lengthwise. Oil a large shallow baking pan (13 inches x 17 inches) and sprinkle the salt over its surface. Place the tomatoes, cut side down, on the pan. Bake in the oven for 2 to 2½ hours, or until the tomatoes are deflated, crinkled-looking, and slightly browned.

3. Put all the tomatoes in a food processor, add the pepper, and process briefly. The sauce should be thick and slightly chunky. Store refrigerated.

Makes about 1½ cups.

Spicy Winter Soup with Roasted-Tomato Essence

The standing time in step 3 is essential—it really pulls the flavors together. This soup is warming on a cold gray night!

1 generous tablespoon mild curry powder
3 tablespoons olive oil
1 large onion or 3 small ones, chopped (2 cups chopped)
one 2-inch piece ginger root, peeled and minced
1 carrot, peeled and diced
1 boiling potato (about ½ pound)
pinch of cayenne pepper
¼ cup raisins
1 cup Roasted-Tomato Essence
2 bay leaves
4 whole cloves
3 cups chicken broth, homemade or canned
¼ cup cognac
salt
¼ cup cream plus 2 tablespoons for garnish (optional)

1. In a large stockpot, warm the curry powder in the olive oil for 2 minutes. Add the onions, ginger, and carrot. Cook over low heat for 8 to 10 minutes, stirring occasionally.

2. Peel and dice the potato and add it to the pot along with all the remaining ingredients, except for the salt and cream; and add 3 cups water. Increase heat and bring to a boil. Reduce heat and simmer, uncovered, for 30 minutes.

3. Remove the cloves and bay leaves. Purée the soup in batches in a food processor or blender. Strain each batch

through a sieve into another pot (do not omit this step). Let stand for 30 minutes. Season to taste with the salt. Gently reheat to a bare simmer and stir in the ¼ cup cream, if using. Ladle into soup bowls and drizzle a teaspoon of additional cream in a design in the center of each bowl of soup.

SERVES 6.

Curry Oil

3 tablespoons curry powder
1 cup plus 1 teaspoon canola oil
    or safflower oil

1. Place the curry powder in a small saucepan or skillet and, if desired, warm gently for 3 to 4 minutes, or until the curry aromas start to announce themselves.

2. Whether you've roasted the curry or not, add the cup of oil and warm gently for 4 minutes. Pour into a very clean jar, let cool, cover, and let steep in the refrigerator for 24 to 48 hours. Line a funnel with a paper coffee filter and use a pastry brush to paint the filter with the remaining teaspoon of oil. Pour the Curry Oil into the filter and let it drip through the funnel into a very clean jar or bottle (this will take several hours). Cover or cork tightly and label with the date. Store refrigerated.

Makes about 1 cup.

Grilled Shrimp with Curry Oil

1 pound large shrimp (about 30 shrimp)
⅓ cup Curry Oil
⅛ teaspoon salt
1 lime, cut into quarters, plus lime slices for garnish

1. Soak 10 bamboo skewers in cold water for 30 minutes.

2. Peel and devein shrimp, leaving tails intact. In a glass or ceramic bowl, combine shrimp, Curry Oil, and salt. Marinate, covered, in the refrigerator for 15 to 20 minutes. (NOTE: Shrimp may be left to marinate in the refrigerator for up to 5 hours.)

3. Heat outdoor or stovetop grill, or preheat broiler. Place 3 shrimps on each skewer, and place on hot grill or under broiler. Grill 2 minutes on each side.

4. Squeeze the lime quarters over the shrimp skewers and serve immediately. Garnish with the lime slices.

SERVES 4.

Minted Melon and Prosciutto

This must be one of the world's easiest appetizers. The addition of Mint Oil to this summer favorite will surprise and delight the palate.

6 tablespoons pine nuts
1 honeydew melon
2 tablespoons Mint Oil
¼ pound prosciutto (preferably imported), cut into strips
6 sprigs parsley, for garnish

1. Toast the pine nuts under the broiler. They'll go from pale to burnt in a few seconds, so watch them closely.

2. Halve and seed the melon and cut the flesh away from the peel into chunks, or scoop out the flesh with a melon baller if you prefer. In a large bowl toss the melon with the Mint Oil.

3. Just before serving, toss with the prosciutto. Spoon equal portions of the mixture onto six plates and sprinkle each with 1 tablespoon of the toasted pine nuts. Garnish each plate with a sprig of parsley.

SERVES 6.

Mint Oil

2 ounces fresh mint (about 2 cups leaves), rinsed, patted dry, and allowed to air-dry thoroughly
1 cup plus 1 teaspoon canola oil or safflower oil

I. After discarding the larger stalks from the mint, combine the leaves and the cup of oil in a food processor or blender and process or blend for 10 seconds. Pour into a very clean jar, cover, and let steep in the refrigerator for 24 to 48 hours.

2. Line a funnel with a paper coffee filter and use a pastry brush to paint the filter with the remaining teaspoon of oil. Pour the Mint Oil into the filter and let it drip through the funnel into another very clean jar or bottle (this may take some time). Cover or cork tightly and label with the date. Store refrigerated.

Makes about 1 cup.

Lemon Grass–Star Anise Vinegar

Lemon Grass–Star Anise Vinegar

10 stalks fresh lemon grass (about ½ pound)
16 star anise (or about 4 tablespoons if broken up)
2⅔ cups rice wine vinegar

1. Remove the dried outer leaves from the lemon grass and wash the tender stalks. Using a mallet, rolling pin, or other heavy object, bruise the lemon grass. Cut into ¼-inch pieces.

2. Place lemon grass, star anise, and vinegar in a small saucepan and heat to just below a simmer. Let cool, pour into a very clean jar, cover, label with the date, and let steep in a cool, dark place for 12 to 14 days.

3. Strain through a cheesecloth-lined funnel into a very clean bottle; cover or cork tightly and store in a cool, dark place.

Makes about 2½ cups.

Seared Scallops with Lemon Grass–Star Anise Vinegar

If you happen to have scallop shells for serving, this is the time to whip them out!

½ cup Lemon Grass–Star Anise Vinegar
1 teaspoon soy sauce
1 teaspoon sugar
freshly ground white pepper
4 tablespoons olive oil
½ teaspoon sesame oil
1 pound sea scallops*
4 scallions, sliced diagonally (reserve 2 inches of the green tops for garnish)

1. Combine the vinegar, soy sauce, sugar, and white pepper in a medium bowl. Whisk in 2 tablespoons of the olive oil, followed by the sesame oil.

2. Heat the remaining 2 tablespoons of olive oil in a sauté pan or skillet until hot. Add scallops and scallions and sauté on highest heat for 3 minutes, or until scallops just begin to turn golden. Remove scallops from pan.

3. Pour the vinaigrette into the pan and cook until reduced by half (about 2 minutes). Return the scallops to the pan and warm through for 1 minute. Divide among four plates or scallop shells and garnish with the sliced scallion greens.

SERVES 4.

*Bay scallops may be used, but reduce cooking time by 1 or 2 minutes, since they're smaller.

Shrimp with Black Beans, Lime, and Ginger Oil

If you don't want to make this an opener, serve it as a main-course salad for two.

¾ cup dried black beans

1½ cups chicken stock (homemade or canned)

½ medium onion

1 carrot, peeled and cut in half

¾ pound medium shrimp

1 tablespoon olive oil

salt

2 or 3 pinches hot red pepper flakes

juice of ½ lime (about 1 tablespoon)

2 tablespoons rice vinegar

1 teaspoon soy sauce

3 tablespoons Ginger Oil

½ ripe tomato, peeled, seeded, and diced

2 tablespoons cilantro, snipped into pieces

1 tablespoon chives or scallion tops, chopped very fine

freshly ground black pepper

leaves from 1 head Bibb or red leaf lettuce

½ lime, thinly sliced, for garnish

1. To prepare the beans, wash them and either soak them overnight or pour 2 cups of boiling water on them in a saucepan, boil for 2 minutes, cover tightly, remove from heat, and let stand for 1 hour, then drain. Add chicken stock, onion, carrot, and enough water to cover by 1 inch. Bring to a boil, then simmer, covered, for 40 minutes to 1 hour, or until tender (the cooking time depends on the freshness of the dried beans). Do not overcook.

Ginger Oil

one 4-inch piece ginger root, peeled and chopped into small dice

1 cup plus 1 teaspoon canola oil or safflower oil

1. Combine the ginger and the cup of oil in a saucepan and warm gently for 10 to 12 minutes. Pour into a very clean jar, let cool, cover, and let steep in the refrigerator for 24 to 48 hours.

2. Line a funnel with a paper coffee filter and use a pastry brush to paint the filter with the remaining teaspoon of oil. Pour the Ginger Oil into the filter and let it drip through the funnel into another very clean jar or bottle (this may take some time). Cover or cork tightly and label with the date. Store refrigerated.

Makes about 1 cup.

2. Peel and devein shrimp. Heat the olive oil in a sauté pan or skillet, add the shrimp, salt, and red pepper flakes, and sauté, stirring often, for 3 minutes, until shrimp are opaque. Place in a large bowl, including juices.

3. To prepare vinaigrette: Combine the lime juice, rice vinegar, and soy sauce in a small bowl; whisk in the Ginger Oil drop by drop.

4. Remove the carrot and onion from the beans and discard. Drain the beans. Add the beans, tomatoes, and vinaigrette to the shrimp, along with the cilantro, chives, salt, and freshly ground pepper to taste (be careful not to under-salt). Toss well. Let marinate, refrigerated, for at least 2 hours. Serve chilled or let come to room temperature.

5. To assemble, place 2 or 3 lettuce leaves on each plate and divide the shrimp-and-black-bean mixture among them. Garnish each plate with a slice of lime.

SERVES 4.

Roast Portobello Mushrooms with Porcini Elixir

4 large Portobello mushrooms or 8 small ones
2 tablespoons extra-virgin olive oil or Shallot Oil
¾ cup Porcini Elixir
salt
freshly ground black pepper

1. Preheat oven to 300°F.

2. Gently remove stems from mushrooms and slice stems lengthwise into 4 pieces each. Brush tops of caps and stems all over with oil (this will require about 1 tablespoon of the oil). Place stems and caps in a shallow baking dish (caps should be stem side down) and roast for 25 minutes.

3. While the mushrooms are roasting, place the Porcini Elixir in a saucepan over high heat, bring to a boil, and simmer uncovered until reduced to ¼ cup—it will become almost syrupy. Place reduced Porcini Elixir in a small bowl, whisk in salt and pepper to taste, then whisk in remaining 1 tablespoon of oil.

4. When mushrooms have finished roasting, they should be tender and a little shriveled-looking. Remove the caps to a serving platter, scatter the stems over them, and drizzle the sauce over all. Serve either warm or at room temperature.

SERVES 4.

Porcini Elixir

2 ounces dried porcini mushrooms
(cèpes)
2 cups boiling water
⅛ teaspoon salt

1. Place the mushrooms in a bowl and pour the boiling water over them. Let soak for 30 minutes.

2. Strain the elixir through a cheesecloth-lined strainer into a small saucepan, reserving reconstituted mushrooms for another use. Bring elixir to a boil, reduce heat, add salt, and simmer for 10 minutes. To store, let cool, pour into a very clean jar, cover, and keep refrigerated.

Makes 1¼ cups.

Hearts of Polenta with Wine-Dark Tomato Sauce

The intense wine flavor in this sauce is especially appealing on a cold winter night. Both the polenta and the sauce may be prepared in advance.

For the polenta:
½ teaspoon olive oil
1 teaspoon salt
1½ cups cornmeal
¼ cup finely grated Parmesan cheese
freshly ground pepper

For the sauce:
1 tablespoon olive oil
½ pound sweet Italian sausage
1 small onion, chopped
1 large clove garlic, minced
2 cups canned crushed tomatoes
1 teaspoon chopped fresh rosemary or ½ teaspoon dried
⅔ cup Red Wine Elixir
salt
freshly ground black pepper
½ cup coarsely grated Parmesan cheese, for garnish

1. To make the polenta, grease a shallow Pyrex or enamel baking dish or baking sheet with sides, no smaller than 11 inches x 8 inches and as large as 11 inches x 17 inches, with ½ teaspoon of olive oil. Bring 3 cups of water to a boil with the salt in a medium, heavy-bottomed saucepan. Combine the cornmeal with 1 cup of cold water, whisking it to eliminate lumps, and then pour it all

into the boiling water. Bring all back to a boil, stirring constantly with a wooden spoon. Immediately reduce heat to low-medium, and continue cooking the polenta for 15 to 20 minutes, stirring constantly, until it is very thick and tears away from the side of the pan. Remove from heat and stir in the finely grated Parmesan and the pepper. Pour into the greased baking dish or sheet, spreading it out to meet the edges if necessary. Let cool.

2. To make the sauce, heat the olive oil in a heavy-bottomed saucepan and add the sausage, squeezed out of its casings. Brown the sausage over high heat, breaking it down into crumbly bits as it cooks. When the sausage is completely brown, reduce heat and add the onion. Cook for 5 minutes. Add the garlic and cook for 2 to 3 minutes. Add the canned crushed tomatoes, rosemary, and Red Wine Elixir. Bring to a boil, reduce heat to a simmer, cover, and cook for 40 minutes. Spoon off any fat that may appear on the top of the sauce. Add salt and pepper to taste.

3. Just before serving, preheat the broiler. Use a 2-inch cookie or biscuit cutter to cut the polenta into shapes—hearts are our favorite, but stars, moons, and diamonds work well, too—or just use a knife to cut simple squares. You should be able to get 12 shapes from the smallest-size pan and up to 20 shapes (although they will be thinner) if you have poured the polenta into a larger one. Put the polenta shapes on a baking sheet and put them under the broiler for 3 to 5 minutes, until browned.

4. Gently reheat the sauce, then spoon ½ cup of it onto each plate and top with 3 to 5 polenta shapes. Garnish with a generous helping of coarsely grated Parmesan cheese.

SERVES 4.

*½ ounce fresh sage (½ cup
    chopped leaves)*
2 cups white wine vinegar

1. Rinse and chop the sage
and put it in a very clean
mason jar. Warm the
vinegar until it is warm to
the touch but not hot and
pour it over the herbs. Let
cool, cover, and label with
the date. Let stand in a
cool, dark place for 2 weeks.

2. Strain through a
cheesecloth-lined funnel
into a very clean bottle and
cover or cork tightly. Store
in a cool, dark place.

Makes about 2 cups.

Leeks with Sage Vinaigrette

*When buying leeks for braising, look for those with nice long
white parts, with the frilly bottoms of the roots still intact (removing them makes the leeks lose their freshness).*

**6 leeks, green tops trimmed off (and reserved for making
    Leek Elixir, if desired)**
salt

For the vinaigrette:
2 tablespoons Sage Vinegar
½ teaspoon Dijon mustard
salt
freshly ground pepper
4 fresh sage leaves
⅓ cup extra-virgin olive oil

1. Trim the frilly bottoms from the ends of the leeks. Cut the
   leeks vertically almost all the way down to the base, keeping the root end intact. Make a quarter turn and cut them
   almost all the way down again. Rinse them well in several
   changes of cold water. Put them in a pot large enough to
   accommodate them and add enough water so they are
   nearly submerged. Add about ½ teaspoon salt. Bring the
   water to a boil, reduce heat, and let simmer, uncovered,
   for 20 to 30 minutes, depending on the thickness of the
   leeks. When they are done, a fork inserted into the thickest part of the leek will meet no resistance. Remove the
   leeks to a couple of layers of paper towel and carefully
   blot away the excess water. Transfer to a serving dish.
   (NOTE: You may add the remaining cooking water to any

batch of Leek Elixir you have in your refrigerator or to the batch you might be simmering on the back of the stove.)

2. While the leeks are cooking, make the vinaigrette: Combine the Sage Vinegar, Dijon mustard, salt and pepper to taste, and the sage in the jar of a blender, small food processor, or mini-chop. Blend or process briefly, until the sage leaves are well chopped. Add the olive oil and blend until emulsified.

3. Pour the vinaigrette over the leeks. Let marinate for 1 hour and serve at room temperature.

SERVES 4 TO 6 AS AN OPENER.

Variation:

Leeks with Tarragon Vinaigrette

Prepare the leeks in the same manner but use the following dressing: In a small bowl, whisk together 1½ tablespoons fresh lemon juice, 1 teaspoon Dijon mustard, and salt and pepper to taste. Whisk in ⅓ cup Tarragon Oil, drop by drop, until well emulsified.

Shallot Oil

10 shallots, sliced
½ cup plus 1 teaspoon canola oil
  or safflower oil
½ cup extra-virgin olive oil

1. Combine the shallots, ½ cup canola oil, and the olive oil in a saucepan and gently heat to a bare simmer. Remove from the heat and pour into a clean jar, let cool, cover, and let steep in the refrigerator for 24 to 48 hours.

2. Line a funnel with a paper coffee filter and use a pastry brush to paint the filter with the remaining teaspoon of canola oil. Pour the Shallot Oil into the filter and let it drip through the funnel into another very clean jar or bottle (this may take some time). Cover or cork tightly and label with the date. Store refrigerated.

Makes about 1 cup.

Asparagus with Shallot Vinaigrette

For the vinaigrette:
¼ cup red wine vinegar
1 teaspoon Dijon mustard
3 anchovies
salt
freshly ground pepper
¼ cup Shallot Oil

1½ pounds asparagus, trimmed of woody bottom ends and peeled

1. Place the vinegar, mustard, anchovies, and salt and pepper to taste in the bowl of a food processor and process until the anchovies are smooth. With the motor running, slowly pour in Shallot Oil.

2. Fill a kettle with water, bring to a boil, and salt generously. Place the asparagus in the water and boil, covered, until just tender—4 to 5 minutes for pencil-thin stalks, about 7 to 9 minutes for medium spears, and 10 minutes for thick ones.

3. Remove the asparagus to a platter. Pour the vinaigrette over the asparagus and let marinate at room temperature for 1 hour. Serve chilled or at room temperature.

SERVES 4.

Variation:

Asparagus with Lime Pink Peppercorn Vinaigrette

Prepare the asparagus using the same method, but dress it with the following vinaigrette: Whisk together ¼ cup rice wine vinegar and 2 teaspoons soy sauce, then stir in ⅓ cup Lime Pink Peppercorn Oil.

CHAPTER FIVE

Salads

The salad bowl is the most obvious stage for showing off the talents of infused oils and flavored vinegars. There, drizzled over greens, poured onto bright, crisp vegetables, or tossed with tomatoes, they are the stars. And lest they be relegated to the wings, even essences and elixirs make cameo appearances in the recipes that follow.

Tossed Green Salads and Our Favorite Vinaigrettes

A fresh salad of tossed greens is the part of the meal we look forward to most. Generally, we serve a green salad as an *entr'acte* between the main course and dessert; the texture of the lettuce and the brightness of the vinaigrette cleanse the palate, aid in digestion, and help us make room for that final, sweet course.

Two things will determine the quality of your salad: the lettuce and the vinaigrette.

Lettuce: Most supermarkets have a limited but growing variety of lettuces available. Buttery heads of Boston, ruffled leaves of red and green leaf, pale spears of Belgian endive, dark red radicchio, curly and bitter chicory, bright arugula and watercress, and delicate sweet mâche—any of these may have appeared already in the produce aisle at your market. If not, ask for them. Remember, demand creates supply. The local farmers' market often offers an even more splendid array, such as amaranth leaves, frisée, dandelion greens, and mesclun, that beguiling collection of baby lettuces, herbs, and edible flowers tossed together.

Whether you're at the grocery store or the farmers' market, look for fresh, supple leaves without discoloration. Aim for balance in terms of color, shape, and taste when selecting greens, and consider combining two or more types. When you get the lettuces home, rinse them well in a basin filled with cold water, making sure to dislodge any dirt, grit, or critters. Spin the greens dry in a salad spinner or lay them out to dry on a double thickness of paper towel. Keep them stored in an *open* plastic bag in the vegetable crisper drawer of your refrigerator. That way, every night you can dip into your Greens of the Week bag and toss them with a Vinaigrette du Jour!

Vinaigrettes: We've never understood the allure of bottled "dressing." A vinaigrette is so easy and quick to make; one splash of acid—lemon juice, vinegar, or maybe even wine—some salt and pepper, three splashes of oil, and you've made the world's most elementary and satisfying sauce. A collection of infused oils and flavored vinegars increases the flavor possibilities without your having to chop up herbs each time you make a vinaigrette.

There is a method to making a classic vinaigrette, which is simple once you understand the principles involved. First, combine the salt and pepper with the acid. Don't skimp on the salt and pepper. This is the best time to add the salt, because the acid will dissolve it. Next, many vinaigrette recipes call for adding Dijon mustard—this acts as an emulsifier (more about that in a minute). Make sure it is well mixed with the acid and the seasonings. Finally, add the oil, and this is the important part. Add it *drop by drop, whisking until the oil and vinegar are broken into tiny droplets and well mixed with each other.* You will know when you have whisked them enough because the mixture will be opaque and milky. This is called an "emulsion." The oil and vinegar, which normally refuse to mix, are in a temporary truce, because their droplets are too small to separate into two big pools. Salt, pepper, and mustard are truce keepers, helping to keep the emulsion stable until the vinaigrette has been eaten. Happily, they add flavor, too. (Commercial bottled dressings use gum and other peculiar ingredients to stabilize their emulsions.) It is possible, however, to emulsify without the addition of mustard—simply be vigilant about drizzling the oil in *literally* drop by drop and whisking vigorously. If you prepare a vinaigrette ahead of time and find it has separated, just give it a few strokes with the whisk.

To be sure, many chefs are now touting nonemulsified sauces, where the oil and the vinegar remain separate. This has become especially popular since flavored and infused oils arrived on the scene. Some vinaigrettes are simply more interesting visually if left unemulsified—the bright amethyst of Opal Basil Vinegar suspended in the emerald green of Basil Oil, for example, is striking on a white salad plate.

As for ingredients, standard proportions for a vinaigrette are one part vinegar to three parts oil. But once you feel comfortable with the process, feel free to play with the proportions and ingredients. Toss the salad with the vinaigrette just before serving so the leaves don't become soggy and wilted.

And don't limit your use of vinaigrettes to salads—they're fabulous for instantly dressing up grilled or simply sautéed fish, poultry, and meat. We've included many such recipes, but go ahead and try different combinations as they strike your fancy.

Our Favorite Vinaigrettes

Lemon–Basil–Black Pepper Vinaigrette

1½ tablespoons fresh lemon juice
1 tablespoon red wine vinegar (homemade, commercial, or
  Bouquet de Provence, page 53)
¼ teaspoon salt
¾ teaspoon cracked black pepper
3 tablespoons Basil Oil

Shallot Oil Vinaigrette

¼ cup red wine vinegar (homemade, commercial, or Bouquet
  de Provence, page 53)
½ teaspoon grated lemon zest
1 teaspoon Dijon mustard
3 anchovies, mashed
salt
freshly ground pepper
¼ cup Shallot Oil

Tarragon Oil Vinaigrette

1½ tablespoons fresh lemon juice
1 teaspoon Dijon mustard
salt
freshly ground pepper
⅓ cup Tarragon Oil

Sunset Vinaigrette

2 tablespoons Opal Basil Vinegar
salt
freshly ground pepper
¼ cup extra-virgin olive oil

Sage Vinaigrette (make this one in a blender, food
    processor, or mini-chop)
2 tablespoons Sage Vinegar
½ teaspoon Dijon mustard
salt
freshly ground pepper
4 fresh sage leaves
⅓ cup extra-virgin olive oil

Chive Oil–Lemon Juice Vinaigrette

1½ tablespoons fresh lemon juice
salt
freshly ground pepper
¼ cup Chive Oil

Double Basil Vinaigrette

2 tablespoons Opal Basil Vinegar
salt
freshly ground pepper
⅓ cup Basil Oil

Tarragon–Chive Oil Vinaigrette

2 tablespoons Pink Tarragon Vinegar or commercial tarragon
    vinegar
salt
freshly ground pepper
½ teaspoon Dijon mustard
⅓ cup Chive Oil

Côte d'Azur Vinaigrette

2 tablespoons fresh orange juice

1 tablespoon Bouquet de Provence Red Wine Vinegar
   (page 53)

¼ teaspoon salt

½ teaspoon cracked pink peppercorns

3 tablespoons Thyme Oil

Pacific Rim Vinaigrette

1½ tablespoons fresh lime juice

salt

freshly ground pepper

¼ cup Ginger Oil

2 tablespoons finely chopped cilantro (add just before serving)

Rosemary-Orange Vinaigrette

⅔ cup fresh orange juice (about 2 oranges)

salt

freshly ground white pepper

½ cup Rosemary Oil

Southeast Asian Vinaigrette

2 tablespoons Lemon Grass–Star Anise Vinegar

salt

freshly ground pepper

1 tablespoon Basil Oil

1 tablespoon canola oil

Vinaigrette de Campagne

2 tablespoons Bouquet de Provence Red Wine Vinegar
   (page 53) or homemade red wine vinegar

salt

freshly ground pepper

5 tablespoons hazelnut oil or walnut oil

Citrus Chive Vinaigrette

juice of 1½ oranges
juice of 1½ limes
1½ teaspoons grated orange zest
salt
freshly ground pepper
1½ tablespoons honey
⅓ cup Chive Oil

Lime Pink Peppercorn Vinaigrette

¼ cup rice wine vinegar
2 teaspoons soy sauce
⅓ cup Lime Pink Peppercorn Oil

Roasted-Tomato Essence Vinaigrette

2 tablespoons Roasted-Tomato Essence
3 tablespoons white wine vinegar
salt
freshly ground black pepper
3 tablespoons extra-virgin olive oil

Endive and Orange Salad with Chive Oil

Chive Oil

1½ ounces fresh chives, chopped into ½-inch pieces (about 1½ cups)
1 cup plus 1 teaspoon canola oil or safflower oil

I. Combine the chives and the cup of oil in a saucepan and gently heat to a bare simmer. Remove from heat, pour into a food processor or blender, and process for 10 seconds. Pour into a very clean jar, let cool, cover, and let steep in the refrigerator for 24 to 48 hours.

2. Line a funnel with a paper coffee filter and use a pastry brush to paint the filter with the remaining teaspoon of oil. Pour the Chive Oil into the filter and let it drip through the funnel into another very clean jar or bottle (this may take some time). Cover or cork tightly and label with the date. Store refrigerated.

Makes about 1 cup.

This composed salad is stunning to look at and easy to assemble. (Oh, and it tastes marvelous, too!) When buying Belgian endive, look for slender heads that are not too green. For freshness, the grocer should store them in the tissue in which they're shipped.

4 to 5 heads Belgian endive
3 oranges
salt
some crushed pink peppercorns (about 1 tablespoon)
4 ounces Stilton cheese, crumbled
3 tablespoons Chive Oil

1. Rinse the heads of endive and peel the leaves away. (They will fall away easily if you trim a little bit off the bottom. After each layer of leaves peels off, trim a bit more off the bottom until you have removed all the leaves.) Arrange the leaves on six individual plates.

2. Peel the oranges with a sharp paring knife, removing all the white pith as you peel, and cut the orange sections out from between the section walls. Place a section of orange at the heart of each endive leaf. Squeeze what remains of each orange (the section walls) over each plate.

3. Sprinkle the salt, crushed pink peppercorns, and crumbled Stilton over all. Drizzle ½ tablespoon of Chive Oil over each serving.

SERVES 6 AS AN OPENER.

Neo-Classic Caesar Salad

Forgoing the classic Caesar's raw egg, we've added Roasted-Garlic Oil, softer and deeper than the traditional raw garlic. We like it so well we've been known to make a whole meal out of it!

18 slices of baguette, about ¼ inch wide
1 tablespoon plus 1 to 2 teaspoons Roasted-Garlic Oil
1 head Romaine lettuce
5 anchovies, chopped as fine as possible or mashed with a
    mortar and pestle
1 tablespoon fresh lemon juice
2 tablespoons red wine vinegar or, better yet, Bouquet de
    Provence Red Wine Vinegar (page 53)
½ teaspoon Worcestershire sauce
lots of freshly ground black pepper
⅓ cup finely grated Parmesan cheese

1. Preheat the oven to 350°F.

2. Place the baguette rounds on a baking sheet and bake for
   about 10 minutes on each side. Turn off the oven and
   leave them in for a few more minutes to dry out. Using a
   pastry brush, paint each round with a thin layer of the 1 to
   2 teaspoons of Roasted-Garlic Oil.

3. Discard the dark outer leaves of the Romaine lettuce,
   wash and dry the remaining leaves, and tear into bite-size
   pieces.

Roasted-Garlic Oil

3 heads garlic
2 teaspoons canola oil or
    safflower oil
1 cup extra-virgin olive oil or
    ½ cup olive oil and ½ cup
    safflower oil or canola oil

1. Preheat the oven to
400°F.

2. Lightly coat the garlic
heads with 1 of the
teaspoons of canola
oil. Roast for 40 minutes.
Remove from the oven and
let cool enough to handle.

3. With a serrated knife,
split the garlic heads in half
horizontally and squeeze
the roasted garlic paste into
a saucepan. Cover with the
olive oil and warm gently
for 5 minutes. Pour into a
very clean jar, let cool,
cover, and let steep in the
refrigerator for 48 hours.

4. Line a funnel with a
paper coffee filter and use a
pastry brush to paint the
filter with the remaining
teaspoon of canola oil. Pour
the Roasted-Garlic Oil into
the filter and let it drip
through the funnel into
another very clean jar or
bottle (this may take some
time). Cover or cork tightly
and label with the date.
Store refrigerated.

Makes about 1 cup.

4. Place the mashed anchovies in the bottom of a salad bowl, add the lemon juice, vinegar, Worcestershire sauce, and pepper, and whisk to combine. Whisk in the remaining tablespoon of Roasted-Garlic Oil.

5. When ready to serve, put the Romaine leaves and baguette rounds in the salad bowl, toss well to combine with the dressing, add the Parmesan cheese, and toss again to coat the leaves.

SERVES 2 AS A MAIN COURSE, 4 AS AN OPENER.

Essential Flavors

Fresh Tomato Salad with Chèvre and Rosemary Oil

We've had enough of tomatoes with mozzarella. Instead, when our favorite nightshades make their first appearance in the garden or at the farmers' market, we pick up a log of chèvre to serve with them. There are many excellent domestic goat cheeses on the market—try to find a good one produced in your area. If you can find low-acid yellow tomatoes, use them, in combination with the red ones, for a splash of color. All the variations listed below are lovely.

4 garden-fresh summer tomatoes
6 ounces chèvre
salt
freshly ground black pepper
3 tablespoons Rosemary Oil

1. A couple of hours before serving, slice the tomatoes thinly. Using dental floss (that's right, dental floss), slice the log of goat cheese into thin discs. Arrange alternating slices of tomatoes and chèvre on a platter. Sprinkle with salt and pepper. Drizzle the Rosemary Oil over all. Be sure to serve with plenty of crusty French or Italian bread for sopping up all the juices.

SERVES 6 AS AN OPENER.

Variations:

For the Rosemary Oil substitute Basil Oil, Tarragon Oil, Roasted-Garlic Oil, Shallot Oil, or Thyme Oil.

Rosemary Oil

1 ounce fresh rosemary (about
    1 cup leaves), rinsed and dried
1 cup extra-virgin olive oil
1 teaspoon canola oil or safflower
    oil

1. Strip rosemary leaves from the stalks. Combine the leaves and olive oil in a saucepan and warm gently for 5 to 7 minutes. Remove from heat and process in a food processor or blender for 10 seconds. Pour into a very clean jar, let cool, cover, and let steep in the refrigerator for 24 to 48 hours.

2. Line a funnel with a paper coffee filter and use a pastry brush to paint the filter with the teaspoon of canola oil. Pour the Rosemary Oil into the filter and let it drip through the funnel into another very clean jar or bottle (this may take some time). Cover or cork tightly and label with the date. Store refrigerated.

Makes about 1 cup.

Fennel Salad with Roasted-Beet Essence and Orange Zest

Unusual and refreshing, and perfect as an opener for a summer dinner party al fresco.

1 bulb fennel
1 tablespoon Roasted-Beet Essence
1 orange (1 tablespoon of the juice and ¼ of the zest, removed in wide strips with a vegetable peeler)
1 tablespoon fresh lemon juice
½ teaspoon salt
1 tablespoon extra-virgin olive oil or Basil Oil

1. Hold the fennel with the flat, root end toward you, cut a small slice off the narrowest side of the bulb, and roll the fennel over so that it is resting on this flat side. Slice the bulb lengthwise into super-thin shavings, so that you get a variety of unusual, interesting shapes. Rinse them gently and pat dry. Arrange on a large platter or on individual plates.

2. Combine the Roasted-Beet Essence, orange juice, lemon juice, and salt and pour it in a thin, zigzagging stream over the fennel. Drizzle the extra-virgin olive oil onto the fennel in the same manner. With a sharp paring knife, cut the wide strips of orange zest into very thin strips and sprinkle them on top.

SERVES 4 AS AN OPENER.

Warmed Chèvre Salad with Sun-Dried Tomato Elixir

Fabulous as is; spectacular if you happen to have some Thyme Oil or Basil Oil to substitute for the olive oil.

one 6-ounce log of chèvre
freshly ground black pepper
1 tablespoon fresh thyme or chopped fresh basil (if not
**   using Thyme Oil or Basil Oil)**
¼ cup extra-virgin olive oil, Thyme Oil, or Basil Oil
3 cups mesclun (mixed baby lettuces)
2 tablespoons red wine vinegar (commercial, homemade, or
**   Bouquet de Provence Red Wine Vinegar (page 53)**
2 tablespoons Sun-Dried Tomato Elixir
salt

1. Using dental floss, slice the chèvre into 4 equal portions. Place them on a plate and make a slight depression in the center of each, using the back of a teaspoon. Grind pepper over them, sprinkle the fresh herbs on them (if using), and drizzle the oil over all. Marinate for 2 hours or more at room temperature, spooning the accumulated oil over them occasionally.

2. Wash and dry the mesclun and put it in a large bowl.

3. Preheat oven to 275°F.

4. Just before you're ready to serve the salad, use a spatula to move the goat cheese to a baking sheet, being careful to reserve the oil that is left in the plate for the dressing.

Sun-Dried Tomato Elixir

4 ounces sun-dried tomatoes
*   (dry—not preserved in oil)*
5⅓ cups boiling water

1. Place the sun-dried tomatoes in a bowl and pour the water over them. Let steep for 45 minutes.

2. Strain out the reconstituted tomato pieces and reserve them for another use.

3. Place the Sun-Dried Tomato Elixir, which should measure about 4 cups, in a small saucepan, bring to a simmer, and continue simmering, uncovered, until the liquid is reduced by half.

Makes about 2 cups.

Warm the chèvre in the oven just until it starts to melt, about 5 to 10 minutes.

5. Meanwhile, prepare the dressing. Whisk together the vinegar, Sun-Dried Tomato Elixir, salt, and pepper in a small bowl. Whisk in the reserved oil drop by drop until it is all incorporated.

6. To serve, toss the mesclun with the dressing. Divide it among four plates and top each with a portion of the chèvre.

SERVES 4 AS AN OPENER.

Minted Beet Salad

4 medium beets
2 oranges
¼ cup Mint Vinegar
2 teaspoons extra-virgin olive oil
salt
freshly ground black pepper
fresh mint, for garnish, if available

1. Preheat oven to 400°F.

2. Wrap each beet individually in aluminum foil, place in a baking pan, and roast for 1 hour, or until tender when poked with a fork through the foil. Let them cool enough to peel—jackets will slip right off with the help of a sharp paring knife.

3. While beets are still warm, cut them into ½-inch dice and place in a medium bowl. Peel the oranges with a sharp paring knife, removing all the white pith. Cut the segments out from between the membranes, then slice into ½-inch pieces. Add to beets.

4. Add Mint Vinegar to beets and oranges; toss briefly. Add olive oil, salt and pepper, and toss again. (NOTE: May be prepared ahead of time and marinated in the refrigerator overnight.) Garnish with fresh mint, if available.

SERVES 4 TO 6 AS A SIDE DISH.

Mint Vinegar

1 large bunch fresh mint
1 cup white wine vinegar
1 cup red wine vinegar

1. Wash the mint, pat it dry, and strip the leaves off the larger stems. Discard any leaves that are turning black. Place the green leaves in a very clean jar.

2. Combine the vinegars in a saucepan, heat until warm to the touch but not hot, and pour them over the mint. Let cool, cover, label with the date, and let steep in a cool, dark place for 4 days.

3. Strain through a cheesecloth-lined sieve into a very clean bottle, pressing on the mint with the back of a wooden spoon; cover or cork tightly. Store in a cool, dark place.

Makes just under 2 cups.

Bistro Salad

Shallot Oil

10 shallots, sliced
½ cup plus 1 teaspoon canola oil
  or safflower oil
½ cup extra-virgin olive oil

I. Combine the shallots, ½ cup canola oil, and the olive oil in a saucepan and gently heat to a bare simmer. Remove from the heat and pour into a clean jar, let cool, cover, and let steep in the refrigerator for 24 to 48 hours.

2. Line a funnel with a paper coffee filter and use a pastry brush to paint the filter with the remaining teaspoon of canola oil. Pour the Shallot Oil into the filter and let it drip through the funnel into another very clean jar or bottle (this may take some time). Cover or cork tightly and label with the date. Store refrigerated.

Makes about 1 cup.

---

4 sweet Italian sausages (about ⅔ to ¾ pound)

For the vinaigrette:
2 tablespoons red wine vinegar or Bouquet de Provence
  Red Wine Vinegar (page 53)
½ teaspoon Dijon mustard
salt
freshly ground black pepper
3½ tablespoons Shallot Oil

½ pound frisée or curly endive (about 4 cups leaves)
4 ounces Roquefort cheese, crumbled

1. Place sausages in a small skillet just large enough to hold them and add cold water to barely cover. Bring to a boil, turn heat down to medium, and continue cooking until all the water has evaporated. Remove sausages and cut them diagonally into slices about ⅜ inch thick. Heat the fat left in the skillet, then sauté the slices in the fat, flipping them over periodically, until they're browned, about 5 to 6 minutes. Drain on paper towels.

2. To prepare the dressing, combine the vinegar, mustard, salt, and pepper to taste in a small bowl, then whisk in the Shallot Oil drop by drop.

3. Wash, dry, and tear up the frisée or curly endive. (NOTE: Recipe may be prepared ahead of time up to this point and held.)

4. When ready to serve, heat the skillet over a medium flame, add the sausage slices, and reheat them for 1 to 2 minutes. Place the frisée in a salad bowl, scatter the crumbled Roquefort and sausages over it, and toss well with the dressing.

SERVES 4 AS AN OPENER, 2 AS A MAIN COURSE.

Tarragon Oil

2 ounces fresh tarragon (about
    3 cups leaves), rinsed and
    dried
1 cup plus 1 teaspoon canola oil
    or safflower oil

1. Strip the tarragon leaves
away from the larger stalks.
Combine the leaves and the
cup of oil in a saucepan.
Gently heat to a bare
simmer. Remove from heat
and process in a food
processor or blender for
10 seconds. Pour into a
very clean jar, let cool,
cover, and let steep in the
refrigerator for 24 to 48
hours.

2. Line a funnel with a
paper coffee filter and use
a pastry brush to paint the
filter with the remaining
teaspoon of oil. Pour the
Tarragon Oil into the filter
and let it drip through the
funnel into another very
clean jar or bottle (this may
take some time). Cover or
cork tightly and label with
the date. Store refrigerated.

Makes about 1 cup.

Carrot–Celery Root Salad with Tarragon Oil

The classic marriage of carrot and tarragon is joined here by the underrated celery root (celeriac) for a happy ménage à trois.

**1 pound carrots, peeled and shredded in a food processor
    or grated**
**1 celery root, peeled and shredded in a food processor or
    grated**

For the dressing:
2 tablespoons red wine vinegar
1 tablespoon Dijon mustard
salt
freshly ground pepper
2 teaspoons honey
2 tablespoons Tarragon Oil

1. Combine shredded carrots and celery root in a salad bowl.

2. In a small bowl, whisk together the vinegar, mustard, salt, pepper, and honey. Whisk in the Tarragon Oil drop by drop until it's all incorporated. Adjust seasoning, pour onto carrots and celery root, and toss. Let sit for 1 hour before serving at room temperature.

SERVES 8 AS A SIDE DISH.

Essential Flavors

Colorful Grilled Chicken Salad on a Bed of Arugula with Basil Lime Vinaigrette

The vibrant colors and flavors of this warm chicken salad make us think of summer, even in darkest January.

For the vinaigrette:
2 tablespoons fresh lime juice
salt
freshly ground black pepper
3 tablespoons Basil Oil

For the salad:
1 red bell pepper
½ cup fresh orange juice
2 carrots, peeled and cut into matchsticks
1 skinless, boneless chicken breast, split
salt
freshly ground black pepper
2 healthy bunches arugula (about 4 cups), rinsed and dried
2 ounces chèvre

1. Make the vinaigrette: Whisk the salt and pepper into the lime juice and then whisk in the Basil Oil drop by drop.

2. Preheat the broiler. Cut the pepper in half vertically. Place pepper halves, skin side up, under the broiler. Broil until the skins are totally charred. Place charred pepper halves in a paper bag and roll the bag shut. Set aside for 10 to 15 minutes. Remove peppers from paper bag and remove the seeds and charred black skin which should rub off easily.

Basil Oil

2½ to 3 cups fresh basil leaves, loosely packed, rinsed
¾ cup extra-virgin olive oil
½ cup plus 1 teaspoon canola oil or safflower oil

1. Briefly dunk the basil leaves in boiling water and then plunge them into a bowl of ice water. Drain the basil and blot it with a paper towel to remove excess liquid.

2. Combine the basil, olive oil, and ½ cup of the canola oil in a saucepan and warm gently for 8 to 10 minutes. Remove to a food processor; process 30 seconds. Pour into a very clean jar, let cool, cover, and let steep in the refrigerator 24 to 48 hours.

3. Line a funnel with a paper coffee filter and use a pastry brush to paint the filter with the remaining teaspoon of canola oil. Pour the Basil Oil into the filter and let it drip through the funnel into another very clean jar or bottle (this may take some time). Cover or cork tightly and label with the date. Store refrigerated.

Makes about 1 cup.

Do not rinse. Cut into ½-inch diamond shapes, toss with 1 teaspoon of the vinaigrette, and set aside.

3. In a saucepan, heat the orange juice to a boil and add the carrot matchsticks. Reduce heat and simmer until tender, 5 to 7 minutes. Drain.

4. Heat an outdoor or stovetop grill until very hot. Rinse the chicken breast and pat dry. Sprinkle with salt and pepper and grill for 5 to 7 minutes per side, depending on the size of the breast. Remove to a cutting board and carve on the diagonal into small slices, keeping the shape of the breast intact.

5. Mound the arugula on two dinner plates and scatter the carrot matchsticks and roasted red pepper diamonds over each. Place a carved breast on top of each mound and then use dental floss to cut the goat cheese into four slices. Place two slices on top of each breast. Drizzle the vinaigrette over each plate. Grind some pepper over all.

Serve with crusty bread.

SERVES 2 AS A MAIN DISH.

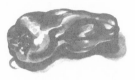

CHAPTER SIX

Pastas and Risottos

Pastas, we've found, are one of the best vehicles for infused oils, and here you'll find lots of recipes that use them to wonderful advantage, along with a few pasta recipes using an essence or elixir. Once you prepare a few of them, you'll quickly see how easy it is to improvise—any type of pasta, simply glossed with an oil infused with herbs, roast garlic, or shallots and tossed with a few grindings of freshly ground pepper and a generous sprinkling of Parmesan cheese, can be sublime. For some ideas, see "Our Favorite Weeknight Pastas" on the following page.

Wonderful as pastas are as a weeknight supper or first course, risottos make for a welcome change. And don't let the twenty minutes of stirring keep you away—we find it has therapeutic value! Besides, there are few dishes that we mortals can do better at home than our favorite restaurants do, but home cooks can show up the pros with risotto, which is almost impossible to prepare in large quantities ahead of time, as our white-hatted friends must. Risottos also make great use of elixirs. Since the idea behind risotto is to encourage the grains of rice to soak up as much liquid as they can, so much the better if the liquid happens to be incredibly flavorful!

To make risotto, you must use imported Arborio rice (regular rice will not work), which has a plump grain with a nice sheen and is available in gourmet shops and Italian groceries.

Our Favorite Weeknight Pastas

Toss your favorite pasta (cooked in plenty of salted water until al dente) with any of the following combinations of ingredients—oil first—plus salt and pepper. Adjust the measurements to suit your own taste and appetite, and feel free to adapt these suggestions according to what you happen to have in your cupboard or refrigerator.

Pasta d'Agosto
Thyme Oil
peeled, seeded, and diced ripe summer tomatoes
chopped garlic
Parmesan cheese (optional)

Pasta Mediterraneo
Roasted-Garlic Oil
pitted and halved black olives (such as kalamata)
chopped parsley
Parmesan cheese

Pasta Via Condotti
Chive Oil
crumbled Gorgonzola cheese
chopped toasted walnuts
sautéed or broiled cherry tomatoes, quartered

Pasta Caravaggio
Rosemary Oil
artichoke hearts (packed in oil), drained and chopped
cracked black pepper
Parmesan cheese

Pasta Paradiso
Basil Oil
sun-dried tomato pieces
Parmesan cheese

Pasta Riccardo
Roasted-Garlic Oil
sautéed escarole
finely grated lemon zest
toasted pine nuts

Pasta Yolande
Shallot Oil
chopped anchovies
hot red pepper flakes

Pasta Piaf
extra-virgin olive oil
Caramelized-Shallot Essence
splash of dry vermouth
chopped parsley
Parmesan cheese

Pasta Mezzanotte
extra-virgin olive oil
Roasted Red Pepper Essence
splash of balsamic vinegar
pitted and halved black olives (such as kalamata)
Parmesan cheese

Pasta Borgia
Basil Oil
Roasted-Tomato Essence
hot red pepper flakes
chèvre (optional)

Penne with Shrimp, Peas, Tomato Bits, and Basil Oil

1 medium tomato, peeled, seeded, and cut into ¼-inch dice*
salt
freshly ground black pepper
2 tablespoons Basil Oil
¾ pound medium or large shrimp
¾ pound dry penne
1 tablespoon olive oil
½ cup fresh peas (frozen are also fine)
⅓ cup shaved Parmesan cheese (shave with a vegetable peeler)

To peel and seed the tomato, plunge it into boiling water for 10 seconds, then plunge it into ice water. The skin will slip off easily. Alternatively, run the back of a knife against the skin all over to loosen the peel. To remove seeds, cut tomato in half horizontally and squeeze gently over the sink.

1. Place the diced tomatoes in a small bowl and add salt and pepper to taste. Add the Basil Oil and toss very gently to combine. (NOTE: This may be done several hours in advance.)

2. Peel and devein shrimp; set aside in the refrigerator.

3. Bring a large amount of salted water to a boil in a pot. Add pasta to boiling water and cook until al dente, about 11 minutes.

4. While pasta is cooking, heat olive oil in a sauté pan. When very hot but not smoking, add shrimp, peas, salt, and pep-

Basil Oil

2½ to 3 cups fresh basil leaves, loosely packed, rinsed
¾ cup extra-virgin olive oil
½ cup plus 1 teaspoon canola oil or safflower oil

1. Briefly dunk the basil leaves in boiling water and then plunge them into a bowl of ice water. Drain the basil and blot it with a paper towel to remove excess liquid.

2. Combine the basil, olive oil, and ½ cup of the canola oil in a saucepan and warm gently for 8 to 10 minutes. Remove to a food processor; process 30 seconds. Pour into a very clean jar, let cool, cover, and let steep in the refrigerator for 24 to 48 hours.

3. Line a funnel with a paper coffee filter and use a pastry brush to paint the filter with the remaining teaspoon of canola oil. Pour the Basil Oil into the filter and let it drip through the funnel into another very clean jar or bottle (this may take some time). Cover or cork tightly and label with the date. Store refrigerated.

Makes about 1 cup.

per. Sauté until shrimp are just opaque, about 3 minutes (do not overcook). Remove from heat.

5. Drain pasta when al dente, place in a large bowl with the shrimp and peas, the tomatoes and Basil Oil, and half the cheese. Toss gently to combine. Garnish with the remaining Parmesan.

SERVES 4 AS A MAIN COURSE, 6 AS AN OPENER.

Orecchiette in Leek Elixir with Spinach

Make sure you set the table with spoons so that everyone can savor the broth down to the last drop.

salt
2 tablespoons olive oil
¼ pound Black Forest ham (ask the butcher or deli person to give you one thick slab), chopped into small dice
1 carrot, peeled and sliced into thin rounds
3½ cups Leek Elixir
¾ pound dry orecchiette ("little ears"), small shells, or other pasta
1 pound fresh spinach leaves, well rinsed and stems removed, chopped into 1- x 3-inch strips
½ cup finely grated Parmesan cheese, plus extra coarsely grated cheese for sprinkling on the finished pasta
freshly ground pepper

1. Bring a large amount of salted water to a boil for the pasta.

2. While the pasta water is coming to a boil, heat the olive oil in a large saucepan and add the ham and carrots. Sauté for 10 minutes, stirring occasionally. Add the Leek Elixir, bring to a boil, and reduce heat to a bare simmer while you cook the pasta.

3. Add the pasta to the boiling water and cook until al dente, about 10 to 12 minutes. Just before draining, add the spinach to the pasta. Drain, reserving ½ cup of the pasta cooking liquid. Add the pasta, spinach, and pasta cooking

Leek Elixir

green parts of 6 to 8 leeks
1 cup dry white wine
3 tablespoons chopped fresh thyme
* or 1½ tablespoons dried*
2 tablespoons black peppercorns
1 teaspoon salt

1. Wash the leek tops, rinsing them thoroughly in at least three or four changes of water to make sure you get rid of all the grit that tends to be lodged between the leaves. Chop them into 1-inch strips. You should have about 8 cups, packed.

2. Combine all ingredients with 6 cups water in a large kettle or stockpot. Bring the water to a boil, reduce the heat, and simmer, partially covered, for 25 minutes. Remove from the heat and let stand 10 minutes.

3. Pour the Leek Elixir through a strainer into a very clean container and let cool. Cover and store refrigerated. Leek Elixir may also be frozen.

Makes about 6 cups.

liquid to the Leek Elixir. The whole combination should be very brothy. Stir in the finely grated cheese and add salt and pepper to taste.

4. Ladle into bowls and sprinkle with the coarsely grated Parmesan.

SERVES 6.

Variation:

Substitute escarole for the spinach.

Essential Flavors

Wild Mushroom Agnolotti with Thyme Oil

Don't be frightened by the idea of making agnolotti—the clever little half-moon stuffed pasta are put together in a snap using gyoza skins, which can be found in the freezer section of many large supermarkets or in just about any Asian grocery. If you don't find gyoza skins, which are round, buy wonton skins, and they'll become whimsical triangles when folded in half.

2 ounces dried porcini*

2 tablespoons unsalted butter

7 tablespoons Thyme Oil or Basil Oil

1 small onion, chopped fine

2 cloves garlic, minced

2 cups roughly chopped shiitakes or other fresh wild
    mushrooms (about 4 ounces)*

salt

freshly ground black pepper

⅔ cup finely grated Parmesan cheese, plus additional for
    sprinkling on the finished pasta

one 12-ounce package gyoza skins or wonton skins,
    defrosted if frozen

1 egg, lightly beaten

*If you prefer to use either all dried mushrooms or all fresh wild ones, simply double the amount of the ones you're using.

1. If using dried porcini, pour 2 cups of boiling water over them in a bowl and let them sit for 30 minutes. Strain out the mushrooms and rinse if they are gritty. Chop them roughly. (NOTE: If you now simmer the remaining liquid for 10 minutes and add salt to taste, you'll have Porcini Elixir!)

Thyme Oil

2 small bunches thyme (about 1 ounce each), rinsed and dried

1⅓ cups extra-virgin olive oil

1 teaspoon canola oil or safflower oil

1. Break up the thyme (no need to remove the leaves from the stems) and bruise it by smashing it with a mallet, rolling pin, or other heavy object. Place the thyme in a small saucepan, cover with the olive oil, and warm gently for 6 to 7 minutes. Pour into a very clean jar, let cool, cover, and let steep in the refrigerator for 48 hours.

2. Line a funnel with a paper coffee filter and use a pastry brush to paint the filter with the teaspoon of canola oil. Pour the Thyme Oil into the filter, and let it drip through the funnel into a very clean jar or bottle (this will take several hours). Cover or cork tightly and label with the date. Store refrigerated.

Makes just over 1 cup.

2. In a medium sauté pan, gently heat the butter and 2 tablespoons of the Thyme Oil, add the onion and garlic, and cook until soft, about 7 to 8 minutes. Add all the mushrooms and salt and pepper to taste and cook for 10 minutes. Let cool slightly.

3. Stir the ⅔ cup Parmesan cheese and 2 more tablespoons of the Thyme Oil into the mushrooms and adjust the seasoning. It should be very flavorful, with plenty of salt and pepper, since there will be a very small amount in each of the agnolotti.

4. Place a gyoza skin on the work surface, and using a teaspoon, place a small spoonful of the mushroom mixture in the center. Brush a little of the beaten egg around half of the periphery, fold the skin in half, and press the edges together to seal. Place on a tray lined with parchment paper or wax paper. Continue until all the filling is used up; when the tray is filled, place another piece of paper over it and continue laying the filled pasta on top. Cover with plastic and place tray in refrigerator until ready to use (see below for instructions on making ahead and freezing).

5. When ready to serve, bring a large kettle of water to a boil; salt well. Drop about one-third of the agnolotti into the water, or just enough so they aren't too crowded; turn down heat so water is boiling very gently. Cook for 3 to 4 minutes, or until the skins are just translucent. Remove with a slotted spoon to a warmed platter. Continue with two more batches.

6. To serve, divide the agnolotti among the plates and drizzle with the remaining Thyme Oil and a grinding of fresh black pepper. Sprinkle with freshly grated Parmesan.

SERVES 6 TO 8 AS AN OPENER, 4 AS A MAIN COURSE.

The agnolotti may be prepared ahead and frozen, wrapped in parchment paper or wax paper to separate them, and stored in plastic freezer bags. To cook them, do not thaw; simply drop them into a large quantity of salted boiling water, let the water return to a boil (4 to 5 minutes), reduce heat, and cook at a gentle simmer for another 2½ to 3 minutes. Remove with a slotted spoon and pick up recipe at step 6.

Pasta Pissaladière

Thyme Oil

2 small bunches thyme (about 1 ounce each), rinsed and dried
1⅓ cups extra-virgin olive oil
1 teaspoon canola oil or safflower oil

I. Break up the thyme (no need to remove the leaves from the stems) and bruise it by smashing it with a mallet, rolling pin, or other heavy object. Place the thyme in a small saucepan, cover with the olive oil, and warm gently for 6 or 7 minutes. Pour into a very clean jar, let cool, cover, and let steep in the refrigerator for 48 hours.

2. Line a funnel with a paper coffee filter and use a pastry brush to paint the filter with the teaspoon of canola oil. Pour the Thyme Oil into the filter and let it drip through the funnel into a very clean jar or bottle (this will take several hours). Cover or cork tightly and label with the date. Store refrigerated.

Makes just over 1 cup.

We've stolen all the toppings off one of our favorite dishes from southern France, the onion tart known as pissaladière, which is usually decorated with a crisscross pattern of anchovies, dotted with niçoise olives, and sprinkled with thyme; slices of tomato sometimes put in an appearance. Here we've combined caramelized onions with oven-roasted tomatoes, anchovies, and olives to lend a deeply roasted note to these ingredients. Thyme Oil provides the perfect Mediterranean exclamation point!

2 tablespoons plus 2 teaspoons olive oil
salt
8 plum tomatoes, thinly sliced (about ¼ inch)
4 medium onions (about 1¼ pounds), thinly sliced
4 anchovies
½ cup niçoise olives, pitted
1 pound dry fusilli
3 tablespoons Thyme Oil
freshly ground black pepper
freshly grated Parmesan cheese (optional)

1. Preheat oven to 250°F.

2. Brush two baking sheets with the 2 teaspoons olive oil, sprinkle salt over them, and lay the tomato slices flat on the sheets. Roast for 1 hour to 1 hour 15 minutes, until the tomatoes are dried out and a little stiff.

3. Meanwhile, heat the 2 tablespoons olive oil in a large sauté pan, add the onions, and sauté over medium-low heat, stirring occasionally. After 15 or 20 minutes, the onions

will start to caramelize, turning a burnished gold color. Turn down the heat to low and continue cooking another 15 minutes. Remove from heat.

4. Just after you start the onions, place the anchovies and pitted olives in a small baking dish. After the tomatoes have been in the oven 30 minutes, place the anchovies and olives in the oven as well. Roast for 30 minutes. Meanwhile, bring a large quantity of salted water to a boil for the pasta.

5. When the tomatoes are done, remove them from the baking sheets with a spatula. Cook the pasta in the boiling water for 10 to 11 minutes, or until al dente. Just before the pasta's done, reheat the onions. Drain the pasta, place in a serving bowl, and add the onions, tomatoes, anchovies, olives, Thyme Oil, and salt and pepper to taste. Toss and serve. Sprinkle with Parmesan cheese, if desired.

SERVES 6 AS AN OPENER, 4 AS A MAIN COURSE.

Capellini with Roasted-Garlic Oil, Eggplant, Roasted Peppers, and Arugula

1 red bell pepper
1 yellow bell pepper
one 1-pound eggplant
4 to 5 tablespoons plus 2 teaspoons Roasted-Garlic Oil
salt
freshly ground black pepper
¾ pound capellini, spaghettini, or other thin dry pasta
1 to 2 bunches arugula, rinsed well and roughly chopped
    (about 2½ cups)
⅓ cup finely grated Parmesan cheese

1. Roast the red and yellow peppers: Preheat the broiler. Cut
the peppers in half vertically. Place pepper halves skin side
up on a broiler tray under the broiler. Broil until the skins
are totally charred. Place charred pepper halves in a paper
bag and roll the bag shut. Set aside for 10 to 15 minutes.
Remove peppers from paper bag, and using a sharp paring
knife, remove the seeds and charred black skin, which
should rub off easily. Chop the peppers into tiny dice, the
size of small peas.

2. While the peppers are steaming in their bag, reduce the
oven heat to 350°F. Peel the eggplant and dice it into
cubes approximately the size of pearls. Put the eggplant in
a baking dish and toss with 2 teaspoons Roasted-Garlic
Oil, 1 teaspoon salt, and ½ teaspoon freshly ground black
pepper. Cover with foil and bake for 25 minutes. Remove
from the oven, toss a couple of times, and combine with
the diced roasted peppers.

3. Bring a large pot of salted water to a boil. When the water is boiling, add the pasta and boil it until it is al dente, about 4 to 6 minutes for capellini. Drain and immediately toss with the 4 to 5 tablespoons Roasted-Garlic Oil. Add the arugula, peppers, and eggplant and toss well. Season well with salt and freshly ground pepper and the Parmesan cheese. Serve immediately.

SERVES 6 AS AN OPENER, 4 AS A MAIN COURSE.

Rosemary Oil

1 ounce fresh rosemary (about 1 cup leaves), rinsed and dried
1 cup extra-virgin olive oil
1 teaspoon canola oil or safflower oil

1. Strip rosemary leaves from the stalks. Combine the leaves and olive oil in a saucepan and warm gently for 5 to 7 minutes. Remove from heat and process in a food processor or blender for 10 seconds. Pour into a very clean jar, let cool, cover, and let steep in the refrigerator for 24 to 48 hours.

2. Line a funnel with a paper coffee filter and use a pastry brush to paint the filter with the teaspoon of canola oil. Pour the Rosemary Oil into the filter and let it drip through the funnel into another very clean jar or bottle (this may take some time). Cover or cork tightly and label with the date. Store refrigerated.

Makes about 1 cup.

Penne with Fresh and Wild Mushrooms and Rosemary Oil

Penne from heaven!

2 ounces dried porcini
2 tablespoons olive oil
½ onion, chopped (about ⅓ cup)
2 cloves garlic, chopped
10 ounces white mushrooms, sliced
½ cup beef broth or Porcini Elixir
½ cup dry white wine
salt
freshly ground black pepper
½ pound penne or other dry pasta
¼ cup Rosemary Oil
⅓ cup finely grated Parmesan cheese, plus additional for sprinkling on finished pasta

1. Pour 2 cups of boiling water over the porcini in a bowl and let them sit for 30 minutes. Strain out the mushrooms and rinse them to remove any grit. Chop mushrooms roughly. (NOTE: If you now simmer the remaining liquid for 10 minutes and add salt to taste, you'll have Porcini Elixir!)

2. Heat the olive oil in a sauté pan, add the onion and garlic, and cook for 5 minutes, until translucent. Add the sliced fresh mushrooms, stir to combine, and cook over medium heat, stirring occasionally, 10 minutes, or until mushrooms have given up their water. Add the porcini, beef broth, white wine, and salt and pepper to taste and cook over low heat for 10 minutes.

3. Meanwhile, bring a large quantity of well-salted water to a boil, add the penne or other pasta, and cook until al dente, about 11 to 12 minutes for penne. Drain.

4. Pour penne into a serving dish, cover with the mushrooms, Rosemary Oil, and ⅓ cup Parmesan, and toss to combine. Sprinkle with additional Parmesan.

SERVES 6 AS AN OPENER, 4 AS A MAIN DISH.

Saffron Elixir

½ teaspoon saffron threads, packed
1 cup boiling water

I. Pour the boiling water
over the saffron threads in
a small bowl. Let steep for
30 minutes. Strain, or leave
threads in for visual interest.

2. If not using immediately,
pour into a very clean bottle
or jar, close or cork tightly,
and store refrigerated.

Makes I cup.

Seafood Risotto with Saffron Elixir

As colorful as it is delicious—with the deep yellow of the saffron, bright green of the peas, indigo of the squid, and pink of the shrimp. Who could resist?

½ pound large or medium shrimp
½ pound squid, cleaned (make sure your fishmonger has
    done this)
4 cups homemade fish or chicken stock, or two 13-ounce
    cans chicken broth plus enough water to make 4 cups
3 tablespoons olive oil
1 medium onion, finely chopped
2 garlic cloves, minced
1½ cups Arborio rice
1 cup dry white wine
salt
freshly ground black pepper
1 cup Saffron Elixir, with or without saffron threads left in
⅔ cup frozen tiny peas, defrosted

1. Shell and devein shrimp. Cut squid bodies into ½-inch
   rings; cut the tentacles in half, or if they are very large, in
   quarters. Refrigerate until ready to use.

2. Heat the stock to simmering in a saucepan; keep hot over
   low heat throughout the entire preparation of the risotto.

3. Heat the olive oil in a heavy-bottomed saucepan. Add the
   onion and cook over medium-low heat for 7 to 8 minutes,
   until soft. Add the garlic and cook for another 2 to 3 minutes. Add the rice, stir with a wooden spoon to coat it with

                                     Essential Flavors

the olive oil, and sauté for 5 minutes, at which point it will start turning slightly golden. Pour in the wine and cook over medium-low heat, stirring all the while, until the liquid is almost completely gone.

4. Pour in a ladleful of stock, set a timer for 10 minutes, and continue stirring until the liquid is almost all absorbed. Continue adding stock by the ladleful and stirring until it's absorbed, until the timer dings, at which point add the seafood. Resume adding stock, one ladleful at a time, and stirring until it's absorbed, until it's all used up. Add salt and pepper, half of the Saffron Elixir, and the defrosted peas; continue stirring and cooking until the liquid is absorbed. Add the remaining Saffron Elixir and stir and cook until it's almost absorbed. The rice grains should be separate yet tender, suspended in the sauce. Adjust seasonings and serve immediately.

SERVES 8 AS AN OPENER, 4 TO 6 AS A MAIN DISH.

Leek Elixir

green parts of 6 to 8 leeks
1 cup dry white wine
3 tablespoons fresh thyme or
 1½ tablespoons dried
2 tablespoons black peppercorns
1 teaspoon salt

I. Wash the leek tops, rinsing them thoroughly in at least three or four changes of water to make sure you get rid of all the grit that tends to be lodged between the leaves. Chop them into 1-inch strips. You should have about 8 cups, packed.

2. Combine all ingredients with 6 cups water in a large kettle or stockpot. Bring the water to a boil, reduce heat, and simmer, partially covered, for 25 minutes. Remove from the heat and let stand 10 minutes.

3. Pour the Leek Elixir through a strainer into a very clean container and let cool. Cover and store refrigerated. Leek Elixir may also be frozen.

Makes about 6 cups.

Risotto with Leek Elixir, Sun-Dried Tomatoes, and Parsley

12 sun-dried tomatoes (dry—not preserved in oil)
½ cup finely chopped parsley
½ cup finely grated Parmesan cheese
¼ teaspoon grated orange zest
3 cups Leek Elixir
2 tablespoons olive oil
½ onion, chopped (about ½ cup)
1 cup Arborio rice
salt
freshly ground black pepper

1. In a small bowl, pour 2½ cups of boiling water over the sun-dried tomato halves and let stand for 20 minutes. Meanwhile, combine the parsley, grated Parmesan cheese, and orange zest in a bowl. Drain the tomatoes, *reserving the liquid,* and chop them into small pieces. In a saucepan, over high heat, reduce sun-dried tomato liquid to 1 cup (or, if you happen to have 1 cup Sun-Dried Tomato Elixir and some already reconstituted sun-dried tomatoes, use those).

2. Add the Leek Elixir to the reduced sun-dried tomato water; heat to simmering, then keep hot over low heat. Meanwhile, heat the 2 tablespoons olive oil in a heavy-bottomed saucepan, add the chopped onion, and sauté over low heat for 2 minutes. Add the rice and sun-dried tomato bits, stir to coat, and turn up the heat to medium-low. Continue cooking for 5 minutes, stirring frequently.

3. Add a ladleful of hot broth to the rice—it will sizzle loudly. Cook, stirring constantly, until the liquid is almost

entirely absorbed, then add another ladleful. Continue in this manner until all but one ladleful of the broth is used. Add half of the parsley-Parmesan mixture, then add the last ladleful of broth, stirring until it is absorbed. The total cooking time after the first broth is added should be 23 to 25 minutes, and the rice should be tender but firm. Remove from heat, stir in the remaining parsley-Parmesan mixture, and season well with salt and pepper.

SERVES 4 AS AN OPENER, 2 AS A MAIN DISH.

Porcini Elixir

*2 ounces dried porcini mushrooms
   (cèpes)*
2 cups boiling water
⅛ teaspoon salt

1. Place the mushrooms in a bowl and pour the boiling water over them. Let soak for 30 minutes.

2. Strain the elixir through a cheesecloth-lined strainer into a small saucepan, reserving reconstituted mushrooms for another use. Bring elixir to a boil, reduce heat, add salt, and simmer for 10 minutes. To store, let cool, pour into a very clean jar, cover, and keep refrigerated.

Makes 1¼ cups.

Risotto with Roast Asparagus and Porcini Elixir

Here the deep flavors of roast asparagus and woodsy mushrooms combine in a heartwarming risotto. If you don't have Porcini Elixir on hand, fear not—you can prepare it while you're roasting the asparagus.

For the roast asparagus:
1 pound asparagus, trimmed of woody bottom ends
salt
1 teaspoon olive oil

For the risotto:
1¼ cups Porcini Elixir
**one 13-ounce can chicken broth plus enough water to make
   2 ¾ cups or 2⅔ cups homemade chicken or veal stock**
2 tablespoons olive oil
4 shallots, minced (about ⅓ cup)
1 cup Arborio rice
**up to ¼ cup reconstituted porcini, cut into bite-size pieces
   (optional)**
**¼ cup finely grated Parmesan cheese, plus additional for
   sprinkling on finished risotto**
2 tablespoons chopped chervil or parsley, for garnish

1. To roast the asparagus, preheat the oven to 425°F. Place the asparagus on a baking sheet, sprinkle salt and 1 teaspoon olive oil over all, and roll them around to cover them with salt and oil. Place in oven and roast until slightly shriveled, about 18 minutes for spears of medium width. Remove from oven, and when cool enough to touch, slice diagonally into 1-inch pieces.

2. To make the risotto, combine the Porcini Elixir with the broth and water or stock in a saucepan; heat to simmering, then keep hot over low heat. Meanwhile, heat the 2 tablespoons olive oil in a heavy-bottomed saucepan, add the shallots, and cook on low heat 2 minutes. Add the rice to the oil and shallots, stir to cover with oil, and turn up the heat to medium-low. Continue cooking rice, stirring frequently for 5 minutes—the rice will turn slightly golden.

3. Add a ladleful of the hot broth to the rice—it will sizzle loudly. Cook, stirring constantly, until the liquid is almost entirely absorbed, then add another ladleful, plus the reconstituted mushrooms, if using. Continue cooking, stirring constantly, until liquid is almost absorbed, then add another ladleful of broth. Continue in this manner until almost all the broth is used, and when you add the last amount of broth, add the asparagus with it. Cook, stirring constantly, until the broth is absorbed; the rice should be tender but firm. Cooking time after the first broth is added should be 23 to 25 minutes. Remove from heat.

4. Stir in ¼ cup Parmesan, adjust seasoning, and divide among plates. Sprinkle with Parmesan and garnish with chervil or parsley.

SERVES 6 AS AN OPENER, 4 AS A MAIN DISH.

Risotto Cakes

When stored overnight in the refrigerator, leftover risotto turns into a gluey mass. Stumped for years about what to do with it, we've finally hit upon something wonderful— risotto cakes. To make them, form leftover risotto into 1-inch-thick patties. Heat a nonstick skillet over medium-high heat until hot. Lay the risotto patties in the skillet and let them sizzle for about 5 minutes, then flip them and cook for another 5 minutes. The cakes should be nicely browned and heated through. Drizzle your favorite flavored vinegar over them, serve with a little salad, and you've got a perfect lunch or light supper.

CHAPTER SEVEN

Main Dishes

On busy weeknights, many of us don't have time to fiddle around in the kitchen, so we turn thankfully to our Pantry of Potential. A piece of fresh steamed fish drizzled with an infused oil, a grilled chicken breast with a quick essence-based sauce, or easy sautéed veal scallops dressed up with a vinaigrette provide a quick, civilized, and flavor-filled end to our day.

In calmer moments, when we want to turn out a more elaborate offering, the Pantry of Potential helps us rise to the occasion with style. An elixir for a pork roast, or an essentially new sauce for Rock Cornish game hens, and all of a sudden we find that cooking an important meal is once again something we look forward to.

Lemon-Herb Oil

1 lemon
1 ounce fresh thyme
1 cup plus 1 teaspoon canola oil
  or safflower oil

I. With a vegetable peeler, peel the yellow zest from the lemon, making sure to leave the white pith on the fruit. Wash the thyme, then break it up and "bruise" it using a mallet, rolling pin, or other heavy object. Put the thyme in a saucepan with the lemon zest and the cup of oil. Warm gently over low heat for 5 minutes. Pour into a very clean jar, let cool, cover, and let steep in the refrigerator for 24 to 48 hours.

2. Line a funnel with a paper coffee filter and use a pastry brush to paint the filter with the remaining teaspoon of oil. Pour the Lemon-Herb Oil into the filter and let it drip through the funnel into another very clean jar or bottle (this may take some time). Cover or cork tightly and label with the date. Store refrigerated.

Makes about I cup.

Grilled Tuna with Lemon-Herb Oil and Tomato-Olive Concasse

We used to love big, fat tuna steaks, charred on the outside and rare on the inside, but we don't live as dangerously as we used to! Using thinner-than-usual steaks allows a shorter-than-usual cooking time, so the steaks remain tender while still being cooked through.

½ cup niçoise, kalamata, or other imported black olives
2 tablespoons olive oil
1 onion, diced
2 ripe tomatoes, peeled, seeded, and cut into small dice
3 tablespoons Lemon-Herb Oil
salt
freshly ground black pepper
four ¾-inch tuna steaks*
1 lemon, half of it thinly sliced for garnish

1. Pit the olives and chop them roughly. Heat the olive oil in a small sauté pan, add the onion, and cook over low heat until soft, about 7 minutes. Remove from heat. Add the tomatoes, olives, 2 tablespoons of the Lemon-Herb Oil, and salt and pepper to taste.

2. Heat a stovetop grill or outdoor grill until very hot. Brush the tuna steaks with the remaining Lemon-Herb Oil, sprinkle with salt and pepper, and grill 2 to 3 minutes on each side (or a little longer if they're thicker than ¾-inch). Place steaks on a serving platter, squeeze a little lemon juice over them, and divide the tomato-olive concasse among them, placing it on top of each steak. Garnish with a slice of lemon.

SERVES 4.

* *Or two 1½-inch tuna steaks, each sliced into 2 thinner steaks.*

Halibut with Rosemary Oil

This is a foolproof way to prepare a great fish. Sautéing a fish and then finishing it in the oven is a favorite method with chefs —and halibut has a marvelous texture and subtle flavor that this cooking method shows off particularly well.

salt
freshly ground black pepper
4 halibut steaks (about 2 pounds total)
3 tablespoons olive oil
1 tablespoon Rosemary Oil
¾ cup chicken stock (homemade or canned broth)
1½ teaspoons best-quality paprika
lemon slices, for garnish

1. Preheat oven to 375°F.

2. Salt and pepper both sides of the steaks. In a skillet or sauté pan large enough to hold all four steaks comfortably, heat the olive oil until it is very hot but not smoking. Sauté the steaks about 3 minutes on each side, or until nicely golden brown. Remove steaks to a shallow baking dish or heatproof platter, carefully spoon a little puddle of Rosemary Oil on top of each, and put them in the oven to finish cooking while you prepare a quick sauce.

3. Turn up the heat under the same skillet you used for the fish and add the chicken stock. Scrape up the browned bits on the bottom with a wooden spoon and cook the stock over high heat to reduce it. When it is reduced by half, stir in the paprika and salt and pepper to taste. Turn

Rosemary Oil

*1 ounce fresh rosemary (about
    1 cup leaves), rinsed and dried*
1 cup extra-virgin olive oil
*1 teaspoon canola oil or safflower
    oil*

1. Strip rosemary leaves from the stalks. Combine the leaves and olive oil in a saucepan and warm gently for 5 to 7 minutes. Remove from heat and process in a food processor or blender for 10 seconds. Pour into a very clean jar, let cool, cover, and let steep in the refrigerator for 24 to 48 hours.

2. Line a funnel with a paper coffee filter and use a pastry brush to paint the filter with the teaspoon of canola oil. Pour the Rosemary Oil into the filter and let it drip through the funnel into another very clean jar or bottle (this may take some time). Cover or cork tightly and label with the date. Store refrigerated.

Makes about 1 cup.

off the heat and strain the sauce into a small pitcher or bowl. (This entire step should take about 3 minutes—and make sure it does, so you don't overcook the fish in the oven!)

4. Remove the halibut to a serving platter and pour the sauce over the fish. Garnish with lemon slices.

SERVES 4.

Soft-Shell Crabs with Citrus-Chive Sauce

Soft-shell crabs are one of our favorite quick summer treats. We like the smallest ones the best—they're the sweetest. They should be alive when you buy them; have the fishmonger clean them for you (which involves killing them), and then get yourself home as fast as you can.

For the sauce:
juice of 1½ oranges
juice of 1½ limes
1½ teaspoons grated orange zest
salt
freshly ground pepper
1½ tablespoons honey
⅓ cup Chive Oil

¼ cup olive oil
12 small soft-shell crabs, or 8 larger ones

1. To prepare the sauce, combine the orange juice, lime juice, and orange zest in a small saucepan. Simmer for 3 minutes; remove from heat and add salt and pepper to taste. Whisk in the honey, then whisk in the Chive Oil drop by drop until incorporated.

2. Heat the olive oil in a large skillet or sauté pan until hot. Sprinkle the soft-shell crabs with salt and pepper, place them in the pan, and sauté for 2½ to 3 minutes on each side.

3. To serve, spoon a portion of sauce on each plate, place two or three crabs overlapping on top, and spoon a little more sauce over them.

SERVES 4.

Chive Oil

1½ ounces fresh chives, chopped into ½-inch pieces (about 1½ cups)
1 cup plus 1 teaspoon canola oil or safflower oil

I. Combine the chives and the cup of oil in a saucepan and gently heat to a bare simmer. Remove from heat, pour into a food processor or blender, and process for 10 seconds. Pour into a very clean jar, let cool, cover, and let steep in the refrigerator for 24 to 48 hours.

2. Line a funnel with a paper coffee filter and use a pastry brush to paint the filter with the remaining teaspoon of oil. Pour the Chive Oil into the filter and let it drip through the funnel into another very clean jar or bottle (this may take some time). Cover or cork tightly and label with the date. Store refrigerated.

Makes about I cup.

Black & White Sesame Salmon

10 stalks fresh lemon grass (about ½ pound)
16 star anise (or about 4 tablespoons if broken up)
2⅔ cups rice wine vinegar

1. Remove the dried outer leaves from the lemon grass and wash the tender stalks. Using a mallet, rolling pin, or other heavy object, bruise the lemon grass. Cut into ¼-inch pieces.

2. Place lemon grass, star anise, and vinegar in a small saucepan and heat to just below a simmer. Let cool, pour into a very clean jar, cover, label with the date, and let steep in a cool, dark place for 12 to 14 days.

3. Strain through a cheesecloth-lined funnel into a very clean bottle; cover or cork tightly and store in a cool, dark place.

Makes about 2½ cups.

The salmon fillets in this dish are spectacular-looking, with their black and white speckled crusts of sesame seeds. If you can't find black sesame seeds, go ahead and use all white ones—it's still beautiful and just as delicious. Conversely, you may want to use only black ones for a dramatic presentation. In any case, the crunchy texture of the crust provides a nice contrast to the moist and tender salmon inside.

For the sauce:
one piece of ginger root 1½ inches long
½ cup Lemon Grass–Star Anise Vinegar
1 teaspoon soy sauce
freshly ground white pepper
3 tablespoons olive oil or peanut oil

1½ pounds salmon fillets (two ¾-pound fillets)
¼ cup black sesame seeds (if unavailable, double the amount of white)
¼ cup white sesame seeds

1. To make the sauce, peel the ginger, slice it vertically as thinly as possible, then stack the slices and cut them into very thin julienne strips. In a small bowl, whisk together the vinegar, soy sauce, and white pepper, then whisk in 1 tablespoon of the oil, drop by drop. Add the ginger strips.

2. Using a sharp knife, remove the skin from the bottom of the salmon fillets if it has been left on. Cut the fillets crosswise into four 6-ounce pieces. Combine the black and

white sesame seeds and pour them onto a dinner plate. Take a salmon fillet and press it into the sesame seeds, covering all exposed surfaces with the seeds. Repeat for the other three fillets.

3. Heat the remaining 2 tablespoons oil in a sauté pan or skillet large enough to hold all the fillets. Sauté them, turning them once, until they are just cooked, about 6 minutes total for fillets from the thin end of the fish and up to 10 minutes total for fillets from the thick end of the fish. To test for doneness, gently insert a small sharp knife into one of them and check to see that the flesh is opaque all the way through, though it will still be a little whiter near the surfaces and more orange in the center. Do not overcook. Sprinkle with salt and freshly ground pepper.

4. To serve, divide the sauce among four plates and place a salmon fillet on top of each.

SERVES 4.

1 lemon
1 ounce fresh thyme
1 cup plus 1 teaspoon canola oil
   or safflower oil

1. With a vegetable peeler, peel the yellow zest from the lemon, making sure to leave the white pith on the fruit. Wash the thyme, then break it up and "bruise" it using a mallet, rolling pin, or other heavy object. Put the thyme in a saucepan with the lemon zest and the cup of oil. Warm gently over low heat for 5 minutes. Pour into a very clean jar, let cool, cover, and let steep in the refrigerator for 24 to 48 hours.

2. Line a funnel with a paper coffee filter and use a pastry brush to paint the filter with the remaining teaspoon of oil. Pour the Lemon-Herb Oil into the filter and let it drip through the funnel into another very clean jar or bottle (this may take some time). Cover or cork tightly and label with the date. Store refrigerated.

Makes about 1 cup.

Lemon Sole Baked in Parchment with Lemon-Herb Oil and Parsley

Lemon-Herb Oil is just the thing to complement a delicate fish such as lemon sole. The preparation is simple yet elegant; the dramatic presentation will delight your guests. If you can't find kitchen parchment paper (which is now available in many housewares stores in handy rolls), feel free to use aluminum foil, which works just as well, even if it isn't as pretty.

1½ pounds lemon sole fillets or other sole fillets
½ bunch Italian (flat-leaf) parsley
salt
freshly ground white pepper
4 teaspoons Lemon-Herb Oil

1. Preheat oven to 375°F.

2. If necessary, cut fillets crosswise into serving pieces. There should be between four and eight altogether, to be evenly divided among four parchment packages.

3. Wash the parsley and let it drain but do not dry it too well (you want the steam in the package). Grab the bunch by the stems and twist them off close to the leaves in a big handful. Save the stems for use in a bouquet garni or sauce, as they're very flavorful.

4. Cut a piece of kitchen parchment about 11 x 14 inches. With the sheet lying vertically in front of you, place one or two fillets (one serving size) horizontally across the middle. Sprinkle well with salt and pepper and drizzle ½ teaspoon of the Lemon-Herb Oil over it. Lay a quarter of the parsley

over the fish and drizzle another ½ teaspoon of Lemon-Herb Oil over it. Take the top and bottom edges of the parchment and bring them together to meet over the fish. Holding them together with one hand, scrunch together both sheets on the right side, and roll the edges away from you to close that side of the package. Do the same with the left. Then roll the top down away from you to seal. The top will be curved, and the package will resemble a closed lunch bag. It must be closed well enough so steam doesn't escape. Repeat for the remaining three packages.

5. Place the packages on a baking sheet and slide into the oven. They should be done in 12 to 13 minutes. Check one to make sure—the fish should flake with a fork.

6. To serve, place the still-closed envelopes on a platter or individual plates and let the guests open them at the table for a lovely little puff of aromatic steam.

SERVES 4.

Striped Bass Steamed with Ginger Oil and Scallions

1. Combine the ginger and the cup of oil in a saucepan and warm gently for 10 to 12 minutes. Pour into a very clean jar, let cool, cover, and let steep in the refrigerator for 24 to 48 hours.

2. Line a funnel with a paper coffee filter and use a pastry brush to paint the filter with the remaining teaspoon of oil. Pour the Ginger Oil into the filter and let it drip through the funnel into another very clean jar or bottle (this may take some time). Cover or cork tightly and label with the date. Store refrigerated.

Makes about 1 cup.

Infused oils lend themselves beautifully to steamed fish. This recipe, inspired by a classic Chinese preparation, produces a fish that is at once succulent, flavorful, and elegant. You'll need a bamboo steamer, widely available and inexpensive in just about any Asian grocery or housewares store. If you can't find striped bass, whole sea bass and red snapper also work wonderfully.

2 or 3 whole striped bass, sea bass, or red snapper (about 3 pounds), heads and tails left on
2 to 3 teaspoons salt (1 teaspoon per fish)
1½ tablespoons soy sauce
1 tablespoon sugar
3 tablespoons sake or sherry
6 tablespoons Ginger Oil
1 bunch scallions, thinly sliced on the diagonal, including some of the green part

1. Wash the fish and rub each inside and out with a teaspoon of salt. Make three or four parallel cuts ¼ inch deep on both sides of each fish, so the sauce will steam into them.

2. In a small bowl, combine the soy sauce, sugar, and sake; whisk in the Ginger Oil. Place the fish on the largest plate that will fit inside a large bamboo steamer. Scatter the scallions on top and pour the sauce over them.

3. Fit the plate into the steamer basket, cover the steamer, and set over boiling water in a wok or skillet. Steam until the fish has cooked through, which you can tell by piercing the

thickest part with a chopstick. If the chopstick slides in easily, the fish is done. Start testing after about 12 minutes.

4. When the fish is done, remove it carefully to a platter using a spatula; spoon the sauce that has collected in the plate over the fish. To serve, use a sharp knife to slice each portion, then lift the top fillet gently off the bone. Remove the bone and slice the bottom fillet into portions.

SERVES 4.

Skate Steamed with Chive Oil and Lemon

Skate has long been popular in France, but it's only recently be-gun to appear on restaurant menus in the United States. Chefs love it for its versatility, lovely delicate flavor, and exquisite texture (almost like crabmeat but more tender), but it's also great to cook at home because it's so easy to prepare, inexpensive, and plentiful on both coasts. Ask your fishmonger to fillet it for you if he or she hasn't already—it's a bit of a pain to do it at home. If the preceding recipe didn't convince you to get a bamboo steamer, perhaps this one will.

1½ pounds skate fillets, cut into 4 pieces
salt
freshly ground white pepper
1 tablespoon fresh lemon juice
½ teaspoon balsamic vinegar
½ teaspoon salt
1 teaspoon grated lemon zest
3 tablespoons Chive Oil
lemon slices and parsley, for garnish

1. Find the largest plate that will fit inside a large bamboo
   steamer. Sprinkle the skate fillets with salt and pepper,
   place them on the plate (they'll be overlapping), and fit
   the plate into the steamer basket.

2. In a small bowl, combine the lemon juice, balsamic vinegar,
   salt, and grated lemon zest. Whisk in 1½ tablespoons of the
   Chive Oil. Pour this sauce over the skate on the plate.

3. Fill a sauté pan or wok with about 2 inches of salted water and bring to a boil. Place the steamer basket over it and cover the steamer. Steam the skate for 10 to 12 minutes. It will have a soft, ropy consistency when done and will have lost its slight pinkness.

4. Use a spatula to transfer the skate to a serving platter or individual plates and spoon a little of the sauce left in the plate over it. Drizzle the remaining 1½ tablespoons Chive Oil in equal amounts over each fillet. Garnish with lemon slices and parsley sprigs.

SERVES 4.

1. Preheat the broiler. To roast the peppers, cut them in half vertically, lay them skin side up on a broiler tray, and place them under the broiler until the skins are completely charred. Put them in a paper bag and roll the bag shut. Set aside for 10 to 15 minutes to let the skins loosen.

2. Using a small paring knife, remove the seeds and pull away the inner membranes. Remove the blackened skin. Do not rinse, as this will dilute the flavor.

3. Place the peppers in the bowl of a food processor or blender and purée until smooth.

Makes ¾ cup to 1 cup.

Grilled Chicken Breasts with Roasted Red Pepper–Chive–Lime Sauce

Succulent chicken, bright satiny sauce—perfect for a summer dinner party or a quick meal after a long day at work or play. This easy and elegant dish can be prepared in no time flat if you have Roasted Red Pepper Essence on hand. But even if you have to make up a batch, you can put together this beauty in about a half hour.

½ cup Roasted Red Pepper Essence
1½ tablespoons fresh lime juice
1½ tablespoons fresh orange juice
2 teaspoons soy sauce
freshly ground white pepper
2½ tablespoons Chive Oil
2 whole boneless, skinless chicken breasts, split
   (4 pieces)
salt
lime slices, for garnish (optional)

1. To make the sauce, combine the Roasted Red Pepper Essence, lime juice, orange juice, soy sauce, and pepper in a small bowl. Whisk in 1½ tablespoons of the Chive Oil drop by drop.

2. Using a mallet, rolling pin, or other heavy object, pound the chicken breasts between pieces of wax paper until ⅜ inch to ½ inch thin. Brush each with the remaining Chive Oil on both sides.

3. Heat a stovetop grill or outdoor grill until very hot. Grill the chicken breasts 3 minutes on the first side and 2 min-

utes on the second side. Salt and pepper and remove from grill.

4. To serve, divide the sauce among four plates and lay a chicken breast on top of each plate. Garnish with slices of lime, if desired.

SERVES 4.

Chive Oil

1½ ounces fresh chives, chopped into ½-inch pieces (about 1½ cups)
1 cup plus 1 teaspoon canola oil or safflower oil

1. Combine the chives and the cup of oil in a saucepan and gently heat to a bare simmer. Remove from heat, pour into a food processor or blender, and process for 10 seconds. Pour into a very clean jar, let cool, cover, and let steep in the refrigerator for 24 to 48 hours.

2. Line a funnel with a paper coffee filter and use a pastry brush to paint the filter with the remaining teaspoon of oil. Pour the Chive Oil into the filter and let it drip through the funnel into another very clean jar or bottle (this may take some time). Cover or cork tightly and label with the date. Store refrigerated.

Makes about 1 cup.

Roasted-Tomato Essence

3 pounds fresh plum tomatoes (do not use canned)
1 teaspoon olive oil
½ teaspoon salt
½ teaspoon freshly ground pepper

1. Preheat oven to 250°F.

2. Wash the tomatoes and split them lengthwise. Oil a large shallow baking pan (13 inches x 17 inches) and sprinkle the salt over its surface. Place the tomatoes, cut side down, on the pan. Bake in the oven for 2 to 2½ hours, or until the tomatoes are deflated, crinkled-looking, and slightly browned.

3. Put all the tomatoes in a food processor, add the pepper, and process briefly. The sauce should be thick and slightly chunky. Store refrigerated.

Makes 1½ cups.

Chicken Oven-Braised in Roasted-Tomato Essence with Cinnamon, Bay Leaf, and Onions

We like to serve this in deep midwinter with some Rosemary Citrus Cornbread (see page 170), a green salad, and a bottle of Chianti.

30 small pearl onions, or 1 pint box
one 4-pound chicken, cut into 6 serving pieces, or 2 chicken legs and 2 split breasts
salt
freshly ground black pepper
2 tablespoons safflower oil or other vegetable oil
¾ cup Roasted-Tomato Essence
¾ cup dry red wine
¼ teaspoon hot red pepper flakes (optional)
1 cinnamon stick
1 bay leaf
¼ cup dried currants or raisins

1. Preheat the oven to 350°F.

2. To peel the onions easily, trim off the root ends and drop the onions into a small saucepan of boiling water. Boil for 30 seconds, then drain them and plunge them into a bowl of ice water. The paper skins will slip right off.

3. Rinse and dry the chicken and sprinkle with salt and pepper. Heat the safflower oil in a large flameproof casserole or Dutch oven. When the oil is very hot but not smoking, brown each of the chicken pieces in it. You may have to do this in batches. When all the chicken has been

browned on all sides, put the pieces back into the casserole. (Or brown the chicken in a heavy sauté pan and then transfer to an ovenproof casserole.)

4. Mix together the Roasted-Tomato Essence, wine, and pepper flakes, if using, and pour over the chicken. Tuck the bay leaf and cinnamon stick in the center of the casserole. Strew the onions and currants around, making sure they are covered with some of the sauce. Cover and bake in the oven for 1 hour. Remove bay leaf and cinnamon stick before serving.

SERVES 6.

Rosemary Oil

1 ounce fresh rosemary (about
   1 cup leaves), rinsed and dried
1 cup extra-virgin olive oil
1 teaspoon canola oil or safflower
   oil

1. Strip rosemary leaves
from the stalks. Combine
the leaves and olive oil in a
saucepan and warm gently
for 5 to 7 minutes. Remove
from heat and process in a
food processor or blender
for 10 seconds. Pour into
a very clean jar, let cool,
cover, and let steep in
the refrigerator for 24 to
48 hours.

2. Line a funnel with a
paper coffee filter and use a
pastry brush to paint the
filter with the teaspoon
of canola oil. Pour the
Rosemary Oil into the filter
and let it drip through the
funnel into another very
clean jar or bottle (this may
take some time). Cover or
cork tightly and label with
the date. Store refrigerated.

Makes about 1 cup.

Rosemary Citrus Cornbread

Serve this quick and delicious cornbread with your favorite chili or with Chicken with Roasted-Tomato Essence. If you have any left over the next day, toast it!

2 tablespoons Rosemary Oil, plus extra for greasing the pan
¾ cup yellow cornmeal
¾ cup unbleached all-purpose flour
1 teaspoon baking soda
1 teaspoon cream of tartar
1 teaspoon salt
2 tablespoons sugar
¾ cup sour cream
⅓ cup milk
2 eggs
2 tablespoons safflower oil or canola oil
1 tablespoon grated zest from an orange, a lemon, or a lime, or a combination of these zests

1. Preheat the oven to 425°F.

2. Grease an 8- x 8- x 2-inch pan with a little Rosemary Oil.

3. In a large bowl, sift together the cornmeal, flour, baking soda, cream of tartar, salt, and sugar. In a separate bowl, combine the sour cream, milk, eggs, safflower oil, grated zest and the 2 remaining tablespoons Rosemary Oil, one ingredient at a time, mixing well after each addition.

4. Add the wet ingredients to the dry and mix until all are just combined. Don't overmix. Pour into the prepared pan and pop into the oven for 15 minutes, until springy to the touch. Remove and let cool. Cut into squares.

MAKES 12 SQUARES.

A Tip on Grating Citrus Zest

Everyone hates to grate the zest of citrus fruit— somehow the fruit ends up stuck in the grater's nasty little crevices. But it's a hundred times easier if you use the following trick: Wrap a sheet of plastic wrap (the cheaper, non-name-brand type works best) around the grater or lay a piece of kitchen parchment on top of the appropriate side, and leave it there while you grate as usual. When you peel off the plastic or paper, the zest will come away with it rather than get stuck in the crevices. Remember to turn the fruit as you zest so that none of the bitter white pith is added to your fragrant pile of citrus confetti.

Rosemary Oil

1 ounce fresh rosemary (about 1 cup leaves), rinsed and dried
1 cup extra-virgin olive oil
1 teaspoon canola oil or safflower oil

1. Strip rosemary leaves from the stalks. Combine the leaves and olive oil in a saucepan and warm gently for 5 to 7 minutes. Remove from heat and process in a food processor or blender for 10 seconds. Pour into a very clean jar, let cool, cover, and let steep in the refrigerator for 24 to 48 hours.

2. Line a funnel with a paper coffee filter and use a pastry brush to paint the filter with the teaspoon of canola oil. Pour the Rosemary Oil into the filter and let it drip through the funnel into another very clean jar or bottle (this may take some time). Cover or cork tightly and label with the date. Store refrigerated.

Makes about 1 cup.

Chicken Breasts with Rosemary-Leek Coulis

This spring-green, silky-smooth coulis goes a long way toward jazzing up a plain old chicken breast.

3 leeks
1 tablespoon olive oil
½ cup homemade chicken stock, canned broth, or Leek Elixir
2 tablespoons Rosemary Oil
1 tablespoon fresh lemon juice
salt
freshly ground black pepper
2 whole boneless, skinless chicken breasts, split (4 pieces)
3 tablespoons safflower oil or vegetable oil
1 tablespoon diced red pepper, or 4 sprigs of rosemary, for garnish

1. Chop off the green parts of the leeks and save them to make Leek Elixir, if desired. Rinse the white bottoms of the leek stalks and trim off the frilly ends of the root if they are still attached. Split the leeks lengthwise all the way down the middle and rinse between each layer. Chop each leek horizontally into small half-moon-like sections. Soak in a bowl of cold water to dislodge any remaining grit, changing the water a couple of times.

2. In a large sauté pan with a cover, combine the olive oil, 2 tablespoons water, and the leeks. Cover and cook over low-medium heat for 20 minutes, or until the leeks are soft. Transfer to the bowl of a food processor or blender. Add the chicken stock, Rosemary Oil, and lemon juice

and process or blend until well puréed. Add salt and pepper to taste. Transfer the coulis to a saucepan. (NOTE: It may be held at this stage until you begin to cook the chicken.) Heat the coulis for 5 to 10 minutes over low heat while you cook the chicken breasts.

3. Rinse the chicken breasts, pat them dry with a paper towel, and sprinkle one side with salt and pepper. Heat the safflower oil in a large heavy sauté pan, and when the oil is very hot but not smoking, add the chicken, salted side down. Cook for 4 to 6 minutes (depending on the size of the breasts), or until golden brown, and then flip. Continue cooking the breasts until they are done, approximately 3 to 4 minutes. To serve, spoon some of the coulis onto a plate and place one of the chicken breast halves on top. Garnish the top with a sprinkling of diced red pepper or a sprig of rosemary.

SERVES 4.

Leek Elixir

green parts of 6 to 8 leeks
1 cup dry white wine
3 tablespoons chopped fresh thyme
*   or 1½ tablespoons dried*
2 tablespoons black peppercorns
1 teaspoon salt

1. Wash the leek tops, rinsing them thoroughly in at least three or four changes of water to make sure you get rid of all the grit that tends to be lodged between the leaves. Chop them into 1-inch strips. You should have about 8 cups, packed.

2. Combine all ingredients with 6 cups water in a large kettle or stockpot. Bring the water to a boil, reduce the heat, and simmer, partially covered, for 25 minutes. Remove from the heat and let stand 10 minutes.

3. Pour the Leek Elixir through a strainer into a very clean container and let cool. Cover and store refrigerated. Leek Elixir may also be frozen.

Makes about 6 cups.

Chicken with Leek Elixir and Shallots

A double whammy of savory Leek Elixir and lacy braised shallots. This is wonderful comfort food.

one 3- to 4-pound chicken, cut into 4 serving pieces, or two legs and one split breast
salt
freshly ground pepper
2 carrots, peeled and diced very small
5 to 6 shallots, thinly sliced
1 tablespoon extra-virgin olive oil
1 cup Leek Elixir
1 tablespoon chopped fresh thyme or fresh tarragon, or 1 teaspoon dried thyme or tarragon
¼ cup cognac
4 sprigs fresh thyme, tarragon, or parsley, for garnish

1. Preheat the oven to 400°F.

2. Wash the chicken pieces and dry them thoroughly. Sprinkle generously with salt and pepper.

3. Put the carrots, shallots, and olive oil in the bottom of a flameproof roasting pan just large enough to accommodate all the chicken pieces in one layer without crowding them. Place the chicken pieces, skin side up, on top of the carrots and shallots. Pour in the Leek Elixir, which should come about one-third of the way up the side of the chicken. Sprinkle the thyme over all the chicken and into some of the Leek Elixir.

4. Bake for 55 to 60 minutes, basting every 15 minutes or so. The chicken should be golden brown when done, and the Leek Elixir and shallots should have cooked together and become ever so slightly syrupy.

5. Remove the chicken to a warm platter. Spoon off a couple of tablespoons of fat from the sauce. Add the cognac to the sauce and place over medium heat, scraping off the bits that are stuck to the sides and bottom of the roasting pan and whisking to incorporate. Add salt and pepper to taste. Pour the sauce over the chicken on the platter and serve each piece with a generous helping of the sauce, garnished with a sprig of fresh thyme, tarragon, or parsley.

SERVES 4.

Plum Vinegar

5 or 6 plums
1 cup cider vinegar
1 cup red wine vinegar
2 tablespoons balsamic vinegar

1. To peel plums easily, submerge them in boiling water for 45 seconds, then plunge them into ice water. Slip off skins, cut plums in half, remove pits, and then slice. This should yield about 2 cups of sliced plums.

2. Combine vinegars in a small saucepan and heat until warm to the touch but not hot. Place the peeled fruit in a very large, very clean mason jar and pour vinegar over it. When cool, cover, label with the date, and store in a cool, dark place for 10 to 12 days.

3. Strain through a cheesecloth-lined funnel into a very clean bottle, pressing on the solids with the back of a wooden spoon; cover or cork tightly. Store in a cool, dark place.

Makes about 1¾ cups.

Roast Chicken with Plum Vinegar Pan Sauce

There are few things more satisfying than a good roast chicken. The secret? Frequent basting and a tasty sauce. We use Plum Vinegar to whip up this quick and savory pan sauce. We've had great results with Pink Tarragon Vinegar, Red Wine Elixir, and other elixirs, too (see variations below). Try to get a free-range chicken—it'll remind you of what chicken used to taste like.

one 4-pound free-range chicken
salt
freshly ground black pepper
3 tablespoons olive oil
1 carrot, peeled and sliced
1 small onion, sliced
1 stalk celery, cut into 1-inch pieces
¾ cup Plum Vinegar
1 tablespoon brown sugar
1 tablespoon cold unsalted butter, cut into bits

1. Preheat the oven to 425°F.

2. Rinse the chicken inside and out and pat dry with paper towels. Sprinkle the main cavity with salt and pepper and tie the legs together in front of the cavity, crossing one "ankle" over the other. Rub the chicken all over with some of the olive oil and place it on its side on a rack in a roasting pan. Place pan in oven and roast on this side for 10 minutes.

3. Working quickly so the oven doesn't lose heat, turn the chicken onto its other side (clean oven mitts or tongs are

helpful) and baste—there should be juices accumulated in the pan for this. Roast for 10 minutes on this side.

4. Turn chicken breast up, baste, and roast for 15 minutes, basting once about halfway through. Baste again, salt chicken well, and strew the carrots, onions, and celery around the roasting pan. Reduce oven heat to 350°F. and set a timer for 40 minutes. After a few minutes, check to see if chicken is making gentle sputtering noises. If not, turn oven up to 375°F. Continue roasting chicken, basting every 10 minutes. When timer dings, begin checking for doneness. When chicken is done, the leg should wiggle easily, the juices should run clear when poked with a fork, and an instant-read thermometer should read 170°F. when inserted in the thickest part of the thigh joint. If not done, continue roasting, up to 15 minutes more.

5. Remove the bird from the oven and let it rest on a carving board for 15 to 20 minutes while you make the pan sauce. Drain the fat from the roasting pan, place it over medium-high heat, and pour in ⅓ cup water. Stir with a wooden spoon, scraping up the browned bits that are stuck to the pan, and cook until water is almost evaporated. Add the Plum Vinegar and cook, stirring frequently, until it is slightly reduced and slightly thickened, about 3 to 4 minutes. Whisk in the brown sugar, remove from heat, and whisk in the bits of butter. Adjust seasoning. Strain the sauce through a sieve, pressing down on the vegetables with the back of the wooden spoon to extract all the juices. Carve the chicken and pass the Plum Vinegar pan sauce separately.

SERVES 4.

Variations:

Substitute Red Wine Elixir for the Plum Vinegar and omit the brown sugar.

Substitute Pink Tarragon Vinegar for the Plum Vinegar.

Substitute Opal Basil Vinegar for the Plum Vinegar.

Stuff fresh rosemary between the skin and the breast meat before roasting and substitute ½ cup dry white wine or dry vermouth and ½ cup chicken broth for the Plum Vinegar. Whisk in 2 tablespoons Roasted-Garlic Essence or Caramelized-Shallot Essence after the pan sauce has been strained.

Substitute Blackberry Vinegar for the Plum Vinegar (also nice in combination with fresh rosemary under the skin).

Essential Flavors

Cornish Game Hens with Fig Essence and Cognac

two ¾- to 1-pound Rock Cornish game hens
salt
freshly ground black pepper
1 small onion, finely chopped
1 carrot, peeled and sliced
2 to 3 tablespoons unsalted butter, cut into bits (see step 2)
½ cup Fig Essence
½ cup cognac

1. Preheat the oven to 350°F.

2. Rinse the birds and pat dry. If there is a piece of fat attached to the cavity of either of the birds, remove it and reserve. Sprinkle salt and pepper into the central cavity. Scatter the chopped onion and sliced carrot on the bottom of a roasting pan and toss in the extra bit of fat (if there is no fat, you will need 3 tablespoons of butter instead of 2). Dot the vegetables with the butter. Place the birds on top of the chopped vegetables.

3. Combine the Fig Essence and cognac and mix well. Pour half of this mixture over the two birds, coating them well. Roast the hens for 55 minutes to an hour, or a little longer if your birds are over 1 pound or were very cold to start with. Baste every 10 minutes with the pan juices that accumulate in the roasting pan. If the legs or wings look as though they are getting burned, place a little tent of aluminum foil over them.

4. When the birds are done, remove them from the oven and

Fig Essence

1 pound fresh small black mission figs
2 tablespoons dry white wine
2 tablespoons fresh lemon juice
1 teaspoon vanilla extract or Vanilla-Rum Elixir (page 80)
1 tablespoon sugar
two 1-inch-long strips of lemon zest

1. Wash the figs and chop them coarsely. Combine all ingredients in a saucepan and cook, covered, over medium heat for 10 to 15 minutes, stirring every 4 to 5 minutes.

2. Pour the contents of the saucepan into a food mill or sieve placed over a large bowl. Force the Fig Essence through the food mill or sieve until all that remains behind are the fig skins, lemon zest, and a bit of fig pulp, which you can discard. The Fig Essence in the bowl should be almost jamlike in consistency. Transfer to a clean container and refrigerate for later use or use immediately.

Makes about 1 cup.

the pan and place them on a warm platter. Spoon off the fat from the roasting pan. Add the remaining Fig Essence–cognac mixture and ⅓ cup water to the pan and cook over medium heat, stirring to dissolve all the bits on the bottom of the pan. Strain this sauce through a sieve into a saucepan, pressing down on all the vegetables in the sieve to extract all their juices. Heat the sauce and season to taste with salt and pepper.

5. Place the birds on plates and pour some of the sauce over them. Put the remaining sauce in a small pitcher or sauce-boat for the table.

SERVES 2.

Magret (Duck Breast) with Blackberry Vinegar Sauce

Magret, which is the breast of a moulard duck, is more and more widely available, especially on the East Coast. If you have trouble finding it, you can easily order it by calling D'Artagnan, a leading purveyor of game meats, at 800-DARTAGN. (Otherwise, see the Variation for the more commonly available Muscovy duck breasts, on p. 183.)

The sumptuous richness of the dark meat is well paired with the Blackberry Vinegar sauce, which is spiked with black pepper and smoothed out with chicken stock. Not only that, but it takes less than half an hour to prepare! Pair the magret with Rosemary Potatoes "Sarladaise" and you'll think you're in southwestern France.

1 moulard duck breast, 2½ pounds to 2¾ pounds*
salt
3 tablespoons clarified unsalted butter, or 1½ tablespoons
    unsalted butter and 1½ tablespoons olive oil, or
    2 tablespoons duck fat
3 shallots, chopped
½ cup Blackberry Vinegar or Plum Vinegar
1 teaspoon cracked black pepper
½ cup homemade chicken stock or ¼ cup canned plus
    ¼ cup water
1 teaspoon brown sugar
1 tablespoon cold unsalted butter, cut into bits

1. Preheat oven to 400°F.

2. Cut the duck breast in half where it naturally divides, cut
   four or five parallel diagonal scores about ¼ inch deep

Blackberry Vinegar

12 ounces fresh blackberries
2 cups white wine vinegar or
    champagne vinegar

1. Gently rinse fruit and place it in a very large, very clean mason jar. Heat the vinegar in a saucepan until warm to the touch but not hot and pour over fruit. Let cool completely, then cover tightly, label with the date, and store in a cool, dark place for 10 to 12 days.

2. Strain through a cheesecloth-lined funnel into a very clean bottle, pressing on the solids with the back of a wooden spoon; cover or cork tightly. Store in a cool, dark place.

Makes about 1¾ cups.

---

into the fat, and sprinkle both sides with salt. Heat the clarified butter in a large skillet or sauté pan until it is very hot but not smoking. Place the duck breast halves, fat side down, in the skillet, and let sizzle for about 3 minutes, until they are nicely browned. Turn the pieces over, and let them sizzle 3 minutes on the other side. Transfer them to a roasting pan or baking dish and place them in the oven. Set a timer for 8 to 10 minutes.

3. While the duck is finishing in the oven, prepare a deglazing sauce. Pour out almost all the fat from the skillet and return it to medium heat. Add the shallots and sauté for 2 minutes (do not let them brown). Pour in the Blackberry Vinegar and turn the heat to high. Cook, stirring and scraping up the browned bits in the pan, for 3 to 4 minutes, until the vinegar is reduced by about half. Add the cracked pepper and chicken stock and cook over high heat for another 3 minutes. Whisk in the brown sugar to dissolve and remove pan from heat.

4. Whisk in the bits of cold butter and adjust seasoning.

5. When the timer dings, check doneness of breasts by pressing on the thickest part with your fingertips—the meat should feel springy-firm. Remove the breasts to a carving board and place the smaller edge away from you. Cut slices on the bias and arrange them on a platter or individual plates. When you're finished carving, reheat the sauce briefly, strain it, and pour it over the sliced duck.

SERVES 4.

If moulard duck breasts are not available, substitute 2 whole Muscovy duck breasts, omit the clarified butter or duck fat, and reduce oven cooking time to about 5 minutes, but be sure to test for doneness with your finger, as in step 5.

Roast Duck with Port-Pepper-Sage Sauce

Port-Pepper-Sage Elixir

3 cups ruby port
1 bunch fresh sage, finely chopped
    (about 1 ounce)
3 to 4 grindings of black pepper

I. Combine the ingredients in a saucepan and bring to a boil. Reduce heat and simmer, uncovered, 20 to 25 minutes, until the elixir has been reduced to 2 cups.

2. Strain into a very clean bottle, let cool, cover, and label. Store refrigerated.

Makes 2 cups.

There are two tricks involved in roasting a duck, one of the fattiest and most delicious birds in the world. The first is to coax as much fat as possible out of the bird by poking holes all over it; and the second is to get it beautifully browned by sustaining the high temperature of the initial roasting for much longer than you would for a chicken. The result—a rich and flavorful meat that goes beautifully with the Port-Pepper-Sage sauce—is well worth the small effort.

one 5- to 5½-pound duck
salt
freshly ground black pepper
1 carrot, peeled and sliced
1 onion, sliced
¾ cup Port-Pepper-Sage Elixir
2 teaspoons prepared horseradish
2 tablespoons chopped parsley or chervil

1. Preheat the oven to 425°F.

2. Rinse the duck and pat it dry. Cut off the wing tips, salt and pepper the interior cavity, and tie the legs together in front of the cavity, crossing one "ankle" over the other. With a skewer or the point of a sharp knife, stab the bird all over, especially in the breast, so that the fat will be able to run out during roasting. Put the bird *breast side down* on a rack in a roasting pan. Roast in the oven for 30 minutes.

3. Remove the bird from the oven and pour out the fat that has collected in the pan. (NOTE: If you strain the fat into a

clean container, you can save it for future use.*) Turn the bird *breast side up* and return it to the oven. Roast for 30 more minutes.

4. Reduce oven to 350°F., salt the bird well, scatter the carrots and onions on the bottom of the roasting pan, and roast an additional hour, or until the leg wiggles easily, the juices run clear when pierced with a fork, and an instant-read thermometer inserted into the thickest part of the leg reads 165°F.

5. Set the bird aside to rest and pour off the fat from the roasting pan. Over high heat, add the Port-Pepper-Sage Elixir and horseradish to the pan, whisking to scrape up any browned bits on the bottom of the pan. Cook for 4 to 5 minutes. Strain through a sieve, pressing down on the vegetables to extract their juices. Toss in the parsley. Carve the duck and pass the sauce separately.

SERVES 4.

* *Such as browning the Magret (page 181). Or, to prepare an authentic Potatoes Sarladaise, follow the recipe on page 231 for Rosemary Potatoes "Sarladaise," substituting duck fat for the Rosemary Oil. Or use it to make cassoulet.*

½ ounce fresh sage (½ cup
  chopped leaves)
2 cups white wine vinegar

I. Rinse and chop the sage
and put it in a very clean
mason jar. Warm the
vinegar until it is warm to
the touch but not hot and
pour it over the herbs. Let
cool, cover, and label with
the date. Let stand in a
cool, dark place for
2 weeks.

2. Strain through a
cheesecloth-lined funnel
into a very clean bottle and
cover or cork tightly. Store
in a cool, dark place.

Makes about 2 cups.

Pork Chops Deglazed with Sage Vinegar and Currants

½ cup **Sage Vinegar**
2 tablespoons **dried currants**
salt
freshly ground black pepper
8 **very thin pork chops (about 2 pounds total)**
2 tablespoons **olive oil**
1 tablespoon **cold unsalted butter, cut into bits**
2 tablespoons **chopped chives**

1. Combine the Sage Vinegar and currants in a small bowl; let sit 1 hour.

2. Salt and pepper the pork chops. Heat the olive oil in a skillet or sauté pan large enough to hold half the pork chops. When oil is very hot but not smoking, add 4 of the chops. Turn heat to medium and cook them 3 minutes on the first side, then 2 minutes on the other. Remove to a platter and place in a warm (250°F.) oven while you sauté the remaining chops. Place last 4 chops on the platter in the oven.

3. Keeping heat at medium under the sauté pan, add the sage vinegar and currants. Simmer for 2 minutes, scraping up the browned bits on the bottom of the pan. Remove from the heat, whisk in the butter, and add salt and pepper to taste.

4. Remove the platter from the oven, pour the sauce over the pork chops, and sprinkle the chives over the top.

SERVES 4.

Mustard Pork Chops with Plum Elixir

4 center-cut pork chops, thinly sliced (about ¾ inch thick)
salt
freshly ground black pepper
½ tablespoon olive oil
1 tablespoon Dijon mustard
½ cup Plum Elixir

1. Preheat the oven to 400°F.

2. Sprinkle the chops with salt and pepper. Heat the olive oil in a skillet over high heat until very hot but not smoking. Add the pork chops (you may have to do this in batches) and brown 2 to 3 minutes. Flip the chops and smear the browned side of each with a small dollop of mustard—about ¼ teaspoon per chop. Cook 2 to 3 additional minutes. When the undersides are browned as well, remove the chops to a shallow baking pan.

3. Add the Plum Elixir to the skillet and, over medium heat, scrape up the brown bits on the bottom of the pan. Whisk in the remaining mustard. Pour over the pork chops and put them in the oven for 8 to 10 minutes, or until cooked through (the cooking time will depend on the thickness of the chops). Remove from the oven and serve each chop with several tablespoons of the sauce.

SERVES 4.

Plum Elixir

½ cup dry white wine
⅓ cup Madeira or dry sherry
1 cup dark brown sugar, packed
one 2-inch piece fresh ginger root, peeled and thinly sliced
1 tablespoon black peppercorns
juice and peel of 1 orange
juice and peel of 2 lemons
3 star anise or 1 teaspoon fennel seeds
10 plums, rinsed

1. In a stockpot, combine all ingredients except the plums with 5 cups water. Bring to a boil, stirring occasionally. Reduce heat and simmer 10 minutes.

2. Cut an X at the bottom of each plum and add the plums to the poaching liquid. Poach 10 to 15 minutes, or until the skins start to loosen. With a slotted spoon, remove each plum, dunk it briefly in a bowl of ice water, and remove the skin. Reserve plums for another use. Return skins to the poaching liquid.

3. Continue simmering the poaching liquid another 15 minutes; strain the liquid and discard the solids. Return the liquid to a saucepan and reduce to 2 cups Plum Elixir.

Makes 2 cups.

Shallot Oil

10 shallots, sliced
½ cup plus 1 teaspoon canola oil or safflower oil
½ cup extra-virgin olive oil

I. Combine the shallots, ½ cup canola oil, and the olive oil in a saucepan and gently heat to a bare simmer. Remove from heat and pour into a clean jar, let cool, cover, and let steep in the refrigerator for 24 to 48 hours.

2. Line a funnel with a paper coffee filter and use a pastry brush to paint the filter with the remaining teaspoon of canola oil. Pour the Shallot Oil into the filter and let it drip through the funnel into another very clean jar or bottle (this may take some time). Cover or cork tightly and label with the date. Store refrigerated.

Makes about I cup.

Poached Sausages and Potatoes with Heavenly Vinaigrette

This lovely dish works terrifically well with a variety of infused oils and flavored vinegars. We suggest some of our favorite combinations below, but you can use your imagination to come up with a heavenly duo of your own choosing.

1 pound sweet Italian sausage (or any other type of fresh pork sausage that you happen to see at the butcher or market)
1½ pounds medium red boiling potatoes

For the vinaigrette:
2 to 3 tablespoons Sage Vinegar, Opal Basil Vinegar, Pink Tarragon Vinegar, Bouquet de Provence Red Wine Vinegar, or white wine vinegar
1 teaspoon Dijon mustard
salt
freshly ground black pepper
⅓ cup extra-virgin olive oil, Shallot Oil, Roasted-Garlic Oil, or Chive Oil

¼ cup chopped fresh parsley

1. Prick the sausage links with a fork, put in a saucepan, and add water until barely covered. Heat until just boiling and then reduce heat to a simmer. Simmer for 30 to 35 minutes.

2. Scrub the potatoes but do not peel them. Put them in a large saucepan with enough cold water to cover them and

bring the water to a boil. Cook for 15 to 20 minutes after the boiling begins, or until just tender when pierced with a fork.

3. While the sausages and potatoes are cooking, make the vinaigrette: First combine the vinegar, mustard, salt, and pepper and then whisk in the oil, one drop at a time, until all is emulsified.

4. Drain the potatoes and slice thinly. Remove the sausages from the poaching liquid and slice thinly on the diagonal. Arrange the potatoes in slightly overlapping concentric circles on a platter. Tuck the sausage slices here and there between the potato slices. Pour the vinaigrette over all. Sprinkle with the parsley. Serve immediately.

SERVES 4.

*1 bundle fresh opal (purple) basil
leaves (about 1 ounce)*
2 cups white wine vinegar

I. Rinse the basil and
discard any blackened leaves.
Put all the basil into a very
clean jar. Heat the vinegar
until warm to the touch but
not hot, pour it over the
herbs, and swirl it around
to make sure the herbs are
covered. Let cool, cover,
label with the date, and let
stand in a cool, dark place
for 10 to 14 days.

2. Strain through a
cheesecloth-lined funnel
into a very clean jar or
bottle; cover or cork tightly.
Keep in a cool, dark place.

Makes about 2 cups.

Pork Medallions on a Bed of Parsnip Purée with Opal Basil Vinegar Sauce

Quick, easy, and lustily elegant. The rich and creamy parsnip purée that serves as a bed for the tender pork medallions also works as a perfect foil for Opal Basil Vinegar sauce.

For the parsnip purée:
2 pounds parsnips
salt
3 tablespoons unsalted butter
1 cup hot milk
freshly ground white pepper

For the pork:
1½ pounds pork tenderloin (2 medium tenderloins)
salt
freshly ground black pepper
2 tablespoons clarified unsalted butter or safflower oil
⅔ cup Opal Basil Vinegar
2 tablespoons brown sugar
½ tablespoon cold unsalted butter, cut into bits
2 tablespoons finely chopped parsley
4 parsley sprigs, for garnish

1. Peel the parsnips and cut into 2-inch chunks. Put them in
   a large pot and cover with plenty of salted cold water.
   Bring to a boil and cook until tender, about 10 to 15 minutes. Drain the parsnips, place them in the bowl of a food
   processor with the butter and milk, and process just until
   smooth. (Do not overprocess, or they'll become gummy.)
   Add salt and white pepper to taste. Keep warm in a covered saucepan in a low (250°F.) oven while you prepare
   the pork.

2. Slice the pork into ½-inch medallions and sprinkle both sides with salt and pepper. Heat the clarified butter in a large sauté pan until very hot but not smoking. Add the pork medallions and sauté until nicely browned (about 2½ to 3 minutes per side). This may require two batches. As they're done, remove to a warm platter and cover with foil.

3. Pour out almost all the fat from the sauté pan and place the pan over medium-high heat. Add the Opal Basil Vinegar, turn heat to high, and scrape all the browned bits from the bottom of the pan. Continue cooking about 3 minutes, until vinegar is reduced by about a third. Turn heat down to medium, stir in the brown sugar, and cook another 30 seconds, until the sugar is dissolved. Remove from heat and whisk in the cold butter. Stir in the chopped parsley.

4. Return the pork medallions to the pan, along with any juices that have collected on the platter, and place over medium heat. Cook until heated through, about 1 minute. To serve, divide the parsnip purée among four plates. Lay equal portions of pork medallions on each bed of purée, overlapping them slightly. Pour some of the sauce over each serving. Garnish each plate with a sprig of parsley.

SERVES 4.

Variation:

Substitute Blackberry Vinegar for the Opal Basil Vinegar.

3 cups ruby port
1 bunch fresh sage, finely chopped
(about 1 ounce)
3 to 4 grindings of black pepper

I. Combine the ingredients in a saucepan and bring to a boil. Reduce heat and simmer, uncovered, 20 to 25 minutes, until the elixir has been reduced to 2 cups.

2. Strain into a very clean bottle, let cool, cover, and label. Store refrigerated.

Makes 2 cups.

Roast Pork with Port-Pepper-Sage Elixir

Try this sumptuous roast with Potato Purée (see page 226), using the Chive Oil variation.

salt
freshly ground pepper
1 center-cut (boneless) pork roast, about 4 pounds
2 tablespoons olive oil
2 tablespoons roughly chopped fresh sage, plus 6 to 8 pretty leaves for garnish
2 cups Port-Pepper-Sage Elixir

1. Preheat oven to 350°F.

2. Salt and pepper the pork roast, rub it with olive oil, and smear the chopped sage over it. Place on a rack in a roasting pan, fat side up, and roast for about 1 hour and 25 minutes, or until an instant-read thermometer reads 160°F. Remove to a carving board, place a piece of aluminum foil over it, and let it rest 20 minutes before slicing.

3. While the pork is roasting, bring the Port-Pepper-Sage Elixir to a simmer in a small saucepan. Continue simmering until it is reduced by almost half—it should measure about 1¼ cups. After roast has rested, carve it into slices. To serve, pour a little of the elixir on each plate and place two slices of pork on top. Garnish with a small sage leaf.

SERVES 6 TO 8.

Lamb Chops with Mint Vinegar

This classic flavor trio—lamb, mint, and vinegar—is a fast and easy winner.

1 tablespoon pink peppercorns
⅔ cup Mint Vinegar
1 to 2 tablespoons olive oil
8 rib or loin lamb chops, about 1½ inches thick
salt
freshly ground black pepper
1 teaspoon sugar
½ cup chicken stock, homemade or canned

1. Crush the pink peppercorns with a mallet, rolling pin, or other heavy object. Place them in a small ceramic or glass bowl and add the Mint Vinegar. This may be done several hours before preparation but need not be.

2. Preheat the oven to 400°F.

3. Heat 1 tablespoon of the olive oil in a large skillet until very hot but not smoking. Add the chops and sear them about 3 minutes on each side. They should be nicely browned. (You may need to do this in batches, adding another tablespoon of oil if necessary.)

4. Remove the chops to a roasting pan and salt and pepper them on both sides. Place in the oven to finish cooking while you prepare the sauce, and set a timer for 10 minutes.

5. Turn the heat to medium under the skillet, add the vinegar

Mint Vinegar

1 large bunch fresh mint
1 cup white wine vinegar
1 cup red wine vinegar

1. Wash the mint, pat it dry, and strip the leaves off the larger stems. Discard any leaves that are turning black. Place the green leaves in a very clean jar.

2. Combine the vinegars in a saucepan, heat until warm to the touch but not hot, and pour them over the mint. Let cool, cover, label with the date, and let steep in a cool, dark place for 4 days.

3. Strain through a cheesecloth-lined sieve into a very clean bottle, pressing on the mint with the back of a wooden spoon; cover or cork tightly. Store in a cool, dark place.

Makes just under 2 cups.

with the peppercorns, and scrape up the browned bits on the bottom of the skillet. Turn up the heat to high and let the vinegar reduce almost completely. Stir in the sugar and chicken stock and let reduce until the timer dings.

6. Remove the chops from the oven and set them on a platter. Pour the vinegar–pink peppercorn sauce over them and serve immediately.

SERVES 4.

Essential Flavors

Roast Leg of Lamb with Roasted-Garlic Essence

A rough and ready leg of lamb, redolent with the smell and taste of the Mediterranean.

one 6-pound leg of lamb
½ cup Roasted-Garlic Essence
2 teaspoons ground cumin seeds
4 to 5 anchovy fillets
1 teaspoon dried thyme
2 tablespoons red wine vinegar or Bouquet de Provence
    Red Wine Vinegar (page 53)
salt
freshly ground black pepper
1 carrot, peeled and chopped
1 small onion, chopped
1 tablespoon olive oil
½ cup beef broth or stock
½ cup dry red wine

1. Preheat the oven to 425°F.

2. Trim any excess fat from the leg of lamb but leave the fell (membrane) on the leg. Locate a roasting pan with a rack large enough to accommodate the leg of lamb.

3. In the bowl of a food processor, combine the Roasted-Garlic Essence, ground cumin seeds, anchovy fillets, dried thyme, 2 tablespoons wine vinegar, and salt and pepper. Process until mixed. Set aside 2 to 3 tablespoons of this paste to use later in the pan sauce. Coat the leg of lamb with the remaining paste and sprinkle it with additional

---

Roasted-Garlic Essence

6 heads garlic
1 teaspoon extra-virgin olive oil

1. Preheat oven to 400°F.

2. Place garlic heads in a pan and lightly rub them with oil. Roast for 40 minutes. Remove from the oven and let stand until cool enough to handle.

3. Using a serrated knife, cut the garlic in half horizontally. Squeeze the paste out into a clean bowl. Keep refrigerated and well covered in a glass container.

Makes 1 to 1⅓ cups, depending on the size of the garlic heads.

salt and pepper. Put the chopped carrots, chopped onions, and olive oil in the bottom of the roasting pan, underneath the rack. Place the leg of lamb, fat side up, on the rack and put it in the oven to roast.

4. Roast for 20 minutes at 425°F. After the initial 20 minutes, reduce the heat to 350°F. and, for medium-rare meat, continue to roast for 55 minutes to 1 hour, or until an instant-read meat thermometer inserted in the thickest part of the roast reads 140°F–145°F. Roast it longer (up to 170°F.) if you want your lamb well done.

5. Remove the lamb from the roasting pan and let it sit for 10 to 15 minutes, until it is ready to carve. Spoon off any obvious pools of fat in the roasting pan and scrape any bits of meat off the rack and into the roasting pan. Put the roasting pan over medium-high heat and pour in the beef broth and ½ cup red wine. With a whisk, scrape up the browned bits of meat on the bottom of the pan and press down on the carrot and onion pieces while bringing the pan sauce to a simmer. Add the reserved paste, 1 tablespoon at a time, and continue to stir as the paste is incorporated into the pan sauce. Strain the pan sauce through a sieve into a pre-warmed pitcher. Carve the lamb and serve with the pan sauce.

SERVES 8.

Essential Flavors

Veal Scallops with Rosemary-Orange Sauce

For the sauce:
⅔ cup fresh orange juice (about 2 oranges)
salt
freshly ground white pepper
½ cup Rosemary Oil

For the veal:
4 tablespoons olive oil
1½ pounds veal scallops
salt
freshly ground white pepper

4 rosemary sprigs and 4 orange slices, for garnish

1. To prepare the sauce, strain the orange juice into a small saucepan, bring to a simmer, and simmer for 4 minutes. Place in a bowl, whisk in salt and pepper to taste, then gently stir in Rosemary Oil (do not emulsify).

2. Heat 2 tablespoons of the olive oil in a skillet and when the oil is very hot but not smoking, add veal scallops (do not crowd). Sauté over medium-high heat for 1½ minutes on each side, or until just brown. Keep warm on a platter in a 275°F. oven while sautéing the rest of the scallops, using 2 more tablespoons of the oil for the next batch or batches.

3. After removing the veal, keep heat under pan at medium-high, pour in sauce, and cook for 2 minutes, scraping up any browned bits from the bottom of the pan. To

Rosemary Oil

1 ounce fresh rosemary (about 1 cup leaves), rinsed and dried
1 cup extra-virgin olive oil
1 teaspoon canola oil or safflower oil

1. Strip rosemary leaves from the stalks. Combine the leaves and olive oil in a saucepan and warm gently for 5 to 7 minutes. Remove from heat and process in a food processor or blender for 10 seconds. Pour into a very clean jar, let cool, cover, and let steep in the refrigerator for 24 to 48 hours.

2. Line a funnel with a paper coffee filter and use a pastry brush to paint the filter with the teaspoon of canola oil. Pour the Rosemary Oil into the filter and let it drip through the funnel into another very clean jar or bottle (this may take some time). Cover or cork tightly and label with the date. Store refrigerated.

Makes about 1 cup.

serve, divide the sauce among four plates and place veal scallops on top. Garnish each with a rosemary sprig and an orange slice.

SERVES 4.

Flank Steak Marinated in Plum Vinegar

Many people shy away from flank steak because it looks so tough, all rolled up and sinewy. That's a shame, because it's very flavorful. Letting the meat sit in an acidic marinade for 6 to 8 hours helps immensely to tenderize it.

The leftovers from this dish are excellent in sandwiches and salads. Try it in a sandwich with Roasted Red Pepper Essence.

For the marinade:

½ cup Plum Vinegar

2 tablespoons extra-virgin olive oil, Shallot Oil, or Roasted-Garlic Oil

½ teaspoon salt

½ teaspoon crushed black peppercorns

3 to 4 scallions, sliced, including some of the green part

one 2-pound flank steak

1. In a nonreactive dish, whisk together the ingredients for the marinade.

2. With the point of a sharp knife, stab the flank steak all over on both sides. Put it into the dish with the marinade, making sure it's well coated. Cover and refrigerate for 6 to 8 hours, turning once or twice.

3. Heat an outdoor or stovetop grill until very hot, or pre-heat the broiler. Grill the steak 6 to 8 minutes per side, or broil 2 inches from the flame for 5 to 7 minutes per side. While the steak is cooking, put the marinade in a sauce-

---

Plum Vinegar

5 or 6 plums
1 cup cider vinegar
1 cup red wine vinegar
2 tablespoons balsamic vinegar

1. To peel plums easily, submerge them in boiling water for 45 seconds, then plunge them into ice water. Slip off skins, cut plums in half, remove pits, and then slice. This should yield about 2 cups of sliced plums.

2. Combine vinegars in a small saucepan and heat until warm to the touch but not hot. Place the peeled fruit in a very large, very clean mason jar and pour vinegar over it. When cool, cover, label with the date, and store in a cool, dark place for 10 to 12 days.

3. Strain through a cheesecloth-lined funnel into a very clean bottle, pressing on the solids with the back of a wooden spoon; cover or cork tightly. Store in a cool, dark place.

Makes about 1¾ cups.

---

pan and bring it to a boil, boil for 3 to 4 minutes, reduce heat, and simmer until ready to serve.

4. When the steak is done, let it rest for a few minutes. Then slice it across the grain at a fairly acute angle. Serve the slices topped with the warm marinade.

SERVES 6, 4 IF YOU WANT LEFTOVERS.

Seared Filet Mignon with
Shallot Oil and Raw Shallots

*The fresh piquancy of raw shallots combines with Shallot Oil
for a contemporary spin on an elegant old favorite.*

2 tablespoons black peppercorns
1 teaspoon salt
4 filet mignon steaks
3 tablespoons Shallot Oil
2 shallots, minced
2 tablespoons cognac

1. Using a mallet, rolling pin, or mortar and pestle, crush the
   black pepper. Combine it with the salt and coat the filets
   with the mixture.

2. Select a skillet, preferably cast iron, large enough to hold
   all four steaks. Place it over high heat until a drop of water
   sizzles instantly. Add half the Shallot Oil, allow it to get
   very hot, then add the steaks. Cook them on one side over
   a high flame, 2 to 2½ minutes for rare, 3 minutes for
   medium rare. Turn the steaks over, drizzle the remaining
   Shallot Oil over them, and continue cooking another
   2½ minutes for rare, 3 minutes for medium rare. They
   should be seared nicely brown on both sides.

3. When the second side is finished, leave the steaks in the
   pan over high heat, pour the cognac over them, and simmer over high heat for 1 minute. Remove the steaks to a
   heated serving platter, scatter the raw shallots on top of
   them, and pour any liquid left in the pan over them.

SERVES 4.

Shallot Oil

10 shallots, sliced
½ cup plus 1 teaspoon canola oil
  or safflower oil
½ cup extra-virgin olive oil

1. Combine the shallots,
½ cup canola oil, and the
olive oil in a saucepan and
gently heat to a bare
simmer. Remove from heat
and pour into a clean jar, let
cool, cover, and let steep in
the refrigerator for 24 to
48 hours.

2. Line a funnel with a
paper coffee filter and use a
pastry brush to paint the
filter with the remaining
teaspoon of canola oil. Pour
the Shallot Oil into the
filter and let it drip through
the funnel into another very
clean jar or bottle (this may
take some time). Cover or
cork tightly and label with
the date. Store refrigerated.

Makes about 1 cup.

Veal Stew with Porcini Elixir and Kale

This combines our favorite winter vegetables—kale and turnips—with the deep, woodsy flavor of Porcini Elixir for those nights when a stew is in order.

1 cup unbleached all-purpose flour
salt
freshly ground black pepper
¼ cup olive oil
2 pounds veal stew meat, cut into bite-size chunks
½ cup dry vermouth
1¼ cups Porcini Elixir
3 cups homemade chicken stock, or two 13-ounce cans with enough water added to make 3 cups
4 leeks, well rinsed and sliced into ¼-inch rounds (the tender white part only—save the green parts to make Leek Elixir, if desired)
bouquet garni (celery leaves, bay leaf, sprig of thyme, sprig of parsley, wrapped in cheesecloth and tied with kitchen string)
4 carrots, peeled and roll-cut, or cut on the diagonal into 1-inch pieces
4 medium turnips, cut into 1-inch dice
1 bunch kale (about 1 pound), well rinsed, tough stems removed
grated zest of ½ lemon
juice of ½ lemon
3 tablespoons chopped chives

1. Place flour in a small bowl and add salt and pepper. Heat olive oil in a large kettle or Dutch oven, dredge veal in the

flour, a few pieces at a time, shake off excess, and brown, turning several times. (This may require a few batches.) When the last pieces have finished browning, place all the veal in the kettle, add the vermouth, and cook, uncovered, until the liquid almost disappears. Add the Porcini Elixir, chicken stock, leeks, bouquet garni, and salt and pepper to taste and simmer, partially covered, for 45 minutes.

2. After 45 minutes, add carrots and turnips and continue simmering partially covered. When carrots and turnips have simmered for 25 minutes, add the kale. Continue simmering for another 20 minutes (the stew will have simmered 1½ hours total).

3. While stew is cooking, combine lemon zest and lemon juice in a small saucepan and simmer for 2 minutes. Remove from heat and stir in chives.

4. Remove stew from heat, remove bouquet garni, adjust seasoning, place in a serving dish, and stir in the lemon-chive mixture to finish.

Serve with buttered egg noodles.

SERVES 6.

Roast Veal with Red Wine Elixir and Rosemary

Red Wine Elixir

6 carrots, peeled and cut into small dice

6 stalks celery, cut into small dice

2 medium onions, cut into small dice

2 bottles inexpensive Bordeaux or other soft, drinkable red wine

I. Place the diced vegetables in a saucepan and pour the wine over them. Bring to a simmer and continue simmering, uncovered, over medium-low heat until reduced by two-thirds.

2. Pour the elixir through a strainer into a large measuring cup, pressing on the vegetables with the back of a wooden spoon to extract all the flavor. If you have more than 2 cups, return the elixir to the saucepan and reduce further. If not using immediately, let cool, cover, and store refrigerated in a very clean jar or bottle.

Makes 2 cups.

Ask your butcher to place a thin piece of fat on top of the veal roast for you (veal fat, if possible). If you don't have any Red Wine Elixir on hand, you can make it while the roast is cooking.

one 3-pound veal shoulder roast, boned and rolled

1 to 2 garlic cloves, cut into slivers

5 or 6 sprigs fresh rosemary (about ½ ounce)

salt

freshly ground black pepper

1 cup Red Wine Elixir

1. Preheat the oven to 375°F.

2. Using a small knife, poke slits all over the roast (about 15 to 20 slits) and insert a garlic sliver and a small piece of rosemary in each slit. Sprinkle the roast generously with salt and pepper. If you have rosemary left, chop up ½ teaspoon's worth and save it for the pan sauce.

3. Put the roast on a rack in a roasting pan and place it in the oven. Roast for 1 hour and 15 minutes. Take the roast out of the oven and remove it to a carving board. Let it rest there for 15 to 20 minutes to let the juices retreat back into the meat.

4. While the roast is resting, prepare the sauce. Pour all but 1 tablespoon of the liquid remaining in the pan (if any) into a fat separator or pour into a small bowl and spoon off the fat. Put the pan over medium-high heat and add the Red Wine Elixir and the reserved ½ teaspoon of

chopped rosemary, if using. Cook for 3 to 4 minutes, scraping up the bits that are stuck to the bottom of the pan. Add the defatted liquid, if any. Taste the sauce and correct the salt and pepper. Strain into a warmed sauceboat.

5. To serve, carve the roast into ¼-inch-thick slices and pour some of the sauce over it. Pass any additional sauce in the sauceboat.

SERVES 6.

CHAPTER EIGHT

Complements

S ide dishes are all too often ignored in life, but the role
they play in complementing a main dish is essential.
Here is our collection of vegetable, potato, grain, and
legume dishes, using a variety of infused oils, flavored vinegars, essences, and elixirs. They're sure to inspire the best of
compliments.

Roast Asparagus with Pink Tarragon Vinegar

Pink Tarragon Vinegar

2 bundles fresh tarragon, about
*   1 ounce each*
2 cups white wine vinegar
1 cup red wine vinegar

1. Rinse the tarragon and discard any blackened leaves. Put all the tarragon into a large, very clean jar. Combine the two vinegars in a saucepan and heat until warm to the touch but not hot. Pour the vinegar over the herbs and swirl it around to make sure the herbs are covered. Let cool, cover, label with the date, and let stand in a cool dark place for 10 to 12 days.

2. Strain through a cheesecloth-lined funnel into a very clean jar or bottle; cover or cork tightly. Store in a cool, dark place.

Makes about 3 cups.

The unusual idea of oven-roasting asparagus was suggested to us by Karla Vermeulen, editor of Palate & Spirit *magazine. Roasting brings out the very essence of asparagus; Pink Tarragon Vinegar complements it perfectly.*

1 pound asparagus
salt
½ teaspoon olive oil
2 teaspoons Pink Tarragon Vinegar
freshly ground black pepper

1. Preheat oven to 425°F.

2. Wash asparagus and snap off bottoms. Place them on a baking sheet or in a roasting pan, sprinkle with salt and drizzle with olive oil, and roll the spears around to coat them.

3. Roast 15 to 18 minutes, or until crinkled. Remove asparagus to a platter, drizzle with Pink Tarragon Vinegar, and add salt and pepper to taste. Serve immediately or let cool to room temperature.

SERVES 4.

Grilled Baby Eggplant with Basil Oil Vinaigrette

If you can't find baby eggplant, go ahead and try this with regular-size.

1 pound baby (Italian) eggplants
2 teaspoons salt
1 tablespoon olive oil
freshly ground black pepper
1 tablespoon red wine vinegar
3 tablespoons Basil Oil
salt

1. Cut off tops of eggplants and slice into ¼-inch-thick vertical slices (do not peel). Place in a colander, sprinkle with the 2 teaspoons salt, and toss. Place colander in sink or over bowl, and let stand for 1½ to 2 hours, tossing several times.

2. Rinse eggplant well, drain, place on a thick layer of paper towels, and cover with another thick layer. Press hard on the slices with the heel of your hand. Remove paper towel; slices should be almost translucent. Wherever they still appear opaque and whitish, place a paper towel over the spot and press down.

3. Heat a stovetop grill or outdoor grill until very hot. Brush eggplant slices lightly with olive oil, sprinkle with salt and pepper to taste, and grill 5 to 7 minutes on each side, until evenly browned and a bit floppy. Arrange in overlapping slices on a platter.

Basil Oil

2½ to 3 cups loosely packed fresh basil leaves, rinsed
¾ cup extra-virgin olive oil
½ cup plus 1 teaspoon canola oil or safflower oil

1. Briefly dunk the basil leaves in boiling water and then plunge them into a bowl of ice water. Drain the basil, and blot it with a paper towel to remove excess liquid.

2. Combine the basil, olive oil, and ½ cup of the canola oil in a saucepan and warm gently for 8 to 10 minutes. Remove to a food processor; process 30 seconds. Pour into a very clean jar, let cool, cover, and let steep in the refrigerator for 24 to 48 hours.

3. Line a funnel with a paper coffee filter and use a pastry brush to paint the filter with the remaining teaspoon of canola oil. Pour the Basil Oil into the filter and let it drip through the funnel into another very clean jar or bottle (this may take some time). Cover or cork tightly and label with the date. Store refrigerated.

Makes about 1 cup.

4. Whisk ⅛ teaspoon salt into the vinegar, then whisk in the Basil Oil. Drizzle the vinaigrette over the eggplant slices and let marinate for 1 hour. Serve at room temperature.

SERVES 4.

Fast-as-Lightning Minted Zucchini

This dish can be easily scaled up or down—just count one zucchini per person.

4 medium zucchini
salt
½ to 1 teaspoon freshly ground black pepper
1 tablespoon Mint Oil

1. Thirty minutes before you intend to eat, grate the zucchini in the food processor with the grater blade or using a manual grater. Wrap the grated zucchini in a double thickness of paper towel and set aside for 30 minutes. If you're making a large quantity of zucchini, divide it in half and wrap in two paper-towel bundles or you won't succeed in blotting up all the excess moisture.

2. Heat a sauté pan over medium-high heat. Add the zucchini, salt, pepper, and Mint Oil. Cook the zucchini for 2 to 3 minutes, tossing it with two forks as it cooks, until it is just cooked through. Serve immediately.

SERVES 4.

Variation:

Substitute Thyme Oil for the Mint Oil.

Mint Oil

2 ounces fresh mint (about 2 cups leaves), rinsed, patted dry, and allowed to air-dry thoroughly
1 cup plus 1 teaspoon canola oil or safflower oil

1. After discarding the larger stalks from the mint, combine the leaves and the cup of oil in a food processor or blender and process or blend for 10 seconds. Pour into a very clean jar, cover, and let steep in the refrigerator for 24 to 48 hours.

2. Line a funnel with a paper coffee filter and use a pastry brush to paint the filter with the remaining teaspoon of oil. Pour the Mint Oil into the filter and let it drip through the funnel into another very clean jar or bottle (this may take some time). Cover or cork tightly and label with the date. Store refrigerated.

Makes about 1 cup.

Tarragon Oil

2 ounces fresh tarragon (about 3 cups leaves), rinsed and dried

1 cup plus 1 teaspoon canola oil or safflower oil

1. Strip the tarragon leaves away from the larger stalks. Combine the leaves and the cup of oil in a saucepan. Gently heat to a bare simmer. Remove from heat and process in a food processor or blender for 10 seconds. Pour into a very clean jar, let cool, cover, and let steep in the refrigerator for 24 to 48 hours.

2. Line a funnel with a paper coffee filter and use a pastry brush to paint the filter with the remaining teaspoon of oil. Pour the Tarragon Oil into the filter and let it drip through the funnel into another very clean jar or bottle (this may take some time). Cover or cork tightly and label with the date. Store refrigerated.

Makes about 1 cup.

"Miracle" Cherry Tomatoes

Our trusty editor was so worried that peeling these puppies would be too laborious that she didn't want us to include the recipe. We protested, marching right over to her apartment with a pint of them, insisting that she peel them according to our directions. She peeled two of them and was convinced. As it turns out, she actually enjoyed peeling them so much that once we left, she peeled the rest of them and gobbled them up! Nevertheless, the miracle of these tomatoes isn't the fact that peeling them is so quick and easy (even though the truth is they practically jump out of their skins). Rather, the miracle is that this simplest of preparations yields such a sublimely delicious dish—the whole of the tomatoes, Tarragon Oil, salt, and pepper is truly greater than the sum of its parts.

2 pints cherry tomatoes, stems removed
salt
freshly ground pepper
4 teaspoons Tarragon Oil

1. Preheat oven to 375°F.

2. Fill a large kettle with water and bring to a boil. To loosen the skins of the tomatoes, drop them into the water, leave them for 10 seconds (not longer, or they'll cook), and then drain them and plunge them into ice water.

3. Gently peel the tomatoes—the skins will slip right off—and place them in a baking dish just large enough to hold them in one layer. Sprinkle them with salt and pepper and drizzle the Tarragon Oil over them. Roll them around to

Essential Flavors

make sure they're coated evenly. (NOTE: Tomatoes may be prepared up to this point several hours in advance and covered loosely with foil or plastic. Do not refrigerate.)

4. Just before serving, place them in the oven for 5 minutes, just to warm through. NOTE: If your oven happens to be set on a different temperature to prepare another dish—anywhere between 350° and 425°F.—go ahead and warm the tomatoes at that temperature, adjusting the cooking time slightly according to the temperature (6 minutes at 350° or 4 minutes at 425° should do the trick—5 minutes at in-between temperatures should be fine).

SERVES 6.

Variations:

Substitute Basil Oil, Thyme Oil, Olive Oil, Roasted-Garlic Oil, or Rosemary Oil for the Tarragon Oil.

String Bean Purée with Porcini Elixir

Porcini Elixir

2 ounces dried porcini mushrooms
  (cèpes)
2 cups boiling water
⅛ teaspoon salt

I. Place the mushrooms in a bowl and pour the boiling water over them. Let soak for 30 minutes.

2. Strain the elixir through a cheesecloth-lined strainer into a small saucepan, reserving reconstituted mushrooms for another use. Bring elixir to a boil, reduce the heat, add salt, and simmer for 10 minutes. To store, let cool, pour into a very clean jar, cover, and keep refrigerated.

Makes 1¼ cups.

The combination of string beans and the flavor of wild mushrooms creates a startlingly harmonious flavor.

1 pound string beans, rinsed and ends removed
2 tablespoons cold unsalted butter, cut into bits
⅓ cup Porcini Elixir
salt
freshly ground pepper

1. Boil a big pot of water and salt it very generously. Add beans and cook until tender, about 8 minutes. Do not undercook or they won't purée. Drain.

2. Place the beans in the bowl of a food processor or blender, add the butter, the Porcini Elixir, salt, and pepper, and purée until very smooth. Return the beans to the saucepan, adjust the seasoning, and cover until ready to serve. (NOTE: May be prepared to this point up to 2 hours before serving.)

3. When ready to serve, warm the purée on low heat until bubbling.

SERVES 4.

Braised and Roasted Endives with Orange-Infused Oil

Out of the ordinary and delicious.

6 Belgian endives
2 teaspoons sugar
salt
freshly ground pepper
⅔ cup chicken stock, homemade or canned
2 tablespoons plus 1 teaspoon Orange-Infused Oil*

1. Preheat the oven to 400°F.

2. Rinse the endives, trim off any discolored leaves, and cut them in half vertically. Trim out the conical core at the bottom, using a paring knife. Place cut side up in a nonreactive sauté pan just large enough to hold them, sprinkle with 1 teaspoon of the sugar and salt and pepper, and pour the chicken stock over them. Cover, place over high heat, and when water begins to boil, turn heat to low; simmer, covered, 7 minutes. (NOTE: May be prepared to this point and held until 15 minutes before ready to serve.)

3. Place 1 teaspoon of the Orange-Infused Oil in a baking dish just large enough to hold the endives. Carefully transfer the endives, cut side up, to the baking dish and spoon 2 tablespoons of the stock from the sauté pan over them. Sprinkle with the remaining 1 teaspoon of sugar and drizzle the remaining Orange-Infused Oil over all. Roast for 15 to 20 minutes, until endives are slightly shriveled-looking.

SERVES 6.

* *Not to be confused with commercially available orange oil.*

Orange-Infused Oil

2 oranges
1 cup plus 1 teaspoon canola oil or safflower oil

1. Using a vegetable peeler, peel the zest away from the two oranges, making sure to leave the bitter white pith on the orange. Cut the orange zest into thinner strips, put them into a saucepan with the cup of oil, and warm gently for 5 minutes. Remove to a very clean jar, let cool, cover, and let steep in the refrigerator for 24 to 48 hours.

2. Line a funnel with a paper coffee filter and use a pastry brush to paint the filter with the remaining teaspoon of oil. Pour the Orange-Infused Oil into the filter and let it drip through the funnel into another very clean jar or bottle (this may take some time). Cover or cork tightly and label with the date. Store refrigerated.

Makes about 1 cup.

Spinach Sautéed with Curry Oil

This easy complement is reminiscent of Indian saag *curry.*

2 pounds spinach, stems removed, washed well
2 tablespoons Curry Oil
salt

1. Place the spinach, still dripping wet, in a covered saucepan and cook over medium heat until completely wilted. Drain well in a colander, pressing with the back of a wooden spoon to remove excess moisture. Chop very coarsely.

2. Heat the Curry Oil in the saucepan. Return the spinach to the pan, add salt to taste, and sauté for 3 minutes over medium heat.

SERVES 4.

Variation:

Substitute Cumin Oil for the Curry Oil.

Curry Oil

3 tablespoons curry powder
1 cup plus 1 teaspoon canola oil
or safflower oil

1. Place the curry powder in a small saucepan or skillet and, if desired, warm gently for 3 to 4 minutes, or until the curry aromas start to announce themselves.

2. Whether you've roasted the curry or not, add the cup of oil and warm gently for 4 minutes. Pour into a very clean jar. Let steep in the refrigerator for 24 to 48 hours.

3. Line a funnel with a paper coffee filter and use a pastry brush to paint the filter with the remaining teaspoon of oil. Pour the Curry Oil into the filter and let it drip through the funnel into a very clean jar or bottle (this will take several hours). Cover or cork tightly and label with the date. Store refrigerated.

Makes about 1 cup.

Baked Tomatoes with Cornbread Stuffing and Cumin Oil

An American Southwestern twist on a Provençal standby. If you can't find cornbread stuffing because it's the middle of July, go ahead and substitute plain bread crumbs or make crumbs out of an old batch of homemade cornbread.

5 large fresh vine-ripened summer tomatoes
2 cups packaged cornbread stuffing
½ cup chopped shallots
2 tablespoons fresh thyme leaves
3 tablespoons Cumin Oil
salt
freshly ground black pepper
1 teaspoon extra-virgin olive oil

1. Preheat the oven to 400°F.

2. Split the tomatoes horizontally and squeeze gently to force out the seeds.

3. If your cornbread stuffing is in big dice, crush it down to crumb-size bits with a rolling pin or in a food processor. Toss the cornbread stuffing crumbs, the shallots, and the thyme leaves together in a bowl. Add the Cumin Oil and toss the stuffing mixture or rub it between your hands to make sure all of it is slightly moistened by the oil. Add salt and pepper to taste.

4. Lightly grease one or two shallow gratin pans with the olive oil. Place the tomatoes in the pan or pans and fill each tomato half with the stuffing mixture, forcing it down into

Cumin Oil

3 tablespoons cumin seeds or 3 tablespoons packaged ground cumin
1 cup plus 1 teaspoon canola oil or safflower oil

1. If you are using cumin seeds, roast them over moderate heat in a dry sauté pan for 2 to 3 minutes, grind them in a spice grinder or mini-chop or with a mortar and pestle, and then combine with the cup of oil and gently warm for 5 minutes.

   or

If you are using packaged ground cumin, measure the cumin into a dry, heavy-bottomed saucepan. Gently roast the ground cumin for about 2 minutes over medium heat to release its aroma, then add the cup of oil and gently warm for 5 minutes.

2. Pour into a very clean jar, let cool, cover, and let steep in the refrigerator for 24 to 48 hours. Line a funnel with a paper coffee filter and use a pastry brush to paint the filter with the remaining teaspoon of oil. Pour the Cumin Oil into the filter and let it drip through the funnel into

another very clean jar or bottle (this may take some time). Cover or cork tightly and label with the date. Store refrigerated.

Makes about I cup.

the seed pockets. Bake for about 20 minutes, until the stuffing is browned and the tomatoes are soft.

The tomatoes are best eaten hot, but they may also be served at room temperature.

SERVES 8 TO 10 AS A SIDE DISH, 5 FOR A MAIN-COURSE LUNCH DISH.

Variations:

Substitute Basil Oil, Shallot Oil, Roasted-Garlic Oil, Rosemary Oil, or Thyme Oil for the Cumin Oil.

Roasted-Garlic String Beans

1 red bell pepper

1 pound string beans, rinsed and ends removed

salt

freshly ground black pepper

1 tablespoon Roasted-Garlic Oil

grated zest of 1 lemon

juice of ½ lemon

1. To roast the pepper: Preheat the broiler. Slice pepper in half vertically and place the halves under the broiler, skin side up, until the skins are completely black. Place in a paper bag and roll shut. Let stand for 10 to 15 minutes to let skins loosen, then peel off black part and remove seeds and inner membrane, using a small paring knife. Do not rinse. Slice into string bean–size lengths and set aside.

2. Boil plenty of water in a large saucepan and salt generously. Meanwhile, unless you're fortunate enough to have beautiful little French haricots verts, cut the string beans on the bias into reasonable pieces. Drop them into the boiling water and boil, uncovered, until they're tender yet still crisp, about 3 minutes. Do not overcook. Drain them and refresh under cold running water or plunge into a bowl of ice water.

3. Place the beans in a serving bowl, add the roasted peppers and a generous amount of salt and pepper, and then toss with the Roasted-Garlic Oil. Add the lemon zest and lemon juice and toss again. Try not to eat them all one by one with your fingers before dinnertime. Serve at room temperature.

SERVES 4 TO 6.

Roasted-Garlic Oil

3 heads garlic

2 teaspoons canola oil or safflower oil

1 cup extra-virgin olive oil or ½ cup olive oil and ½ cup safflower oil or canola oil

1. Preheat the oven to 400°F.

2. Lightly coat the garlic heads with 1 of the teaspoons of canola oil. Roast for 40 minutes. Remove from the oven and set aside until cool enough to handle.

3. With a serrated knife, split the garlic heads in half horizontally and squeeze the roasted garlic paste into a saucepan. Cover with the olive oil and warm gently for 5 minutes. Pour into a very clean jar, let cool, cover, and let steep in the refrigerator for 48 hours.

4. Line a funnel with a paper coffee filter and use a pastry brush to paint the filter with the remaining teaspoon of canola oil. Pour the Roasted-Garlic Oil into the filter and let it drip through the funnel into another very clean jar or bottle (this may take some time). Cover or cork tightly and label with the date. Store refrigerated.

Makes about 1 cup.

Blackberry Vinegar

12 ounces blackberries
2 cups white wine vinegar or
    champagne vinegar

1. Gently rinse fruit and place it in a very large, very clean mason jar. Heat the vinegar in a saucepan until warm to the touch but not hot and pour over the fruit. Let cool completely, then cover tightly, label with the date, and store in a cool, dark place for 10 to 12 days.

2. Strain through a cheesecloth-lined funnel into a very clean bottle, pressing on the solids with the back of a wooden spoon; cover or cork tightly. Store in a cool, dark place.

Makes about 1¾ cups.

Braised Red Cabbage with Blackberry Vinegar

This dish has become a Thanksgiving staple for us, giving new life to the tired old cranberry, but don't wait till Thanksgiving to try it.

1 tablespoon fennel seeds
2 tablespoons mustard seeds
2 tablespoons extra-virgin olive oil
1 medium onion, thinly sliced
1 head red cabbage (about 1½ pounds)
1 cup Blackberry Vinegar
⅓ cup honey
1 teaspoon grated orange zest
½ cup dried cranberries
1 bay leaf
salt
freshly ground black pepper

1. Toast the fennel and mustard seeds together in an ungreased sauté pan over medium heat, shaking the pan as you toast the seeds. The mustard seeds will start popping and will turn grayish as they are cooked. Grind the toasted spices in a spice grinder or by hand with a mortar and pestle. In a large kettle, heat the oil, add the onion to it, and cook over low heat for 5 to 10 minutes, until the onion is soft. Add the toasted ground spices to the onions and continue to cook for another 7 minutes, stirring occasionally so the onions do not stick to the bottom of the pan.

2. Meanwhile, quarter the cabbage and cut out the heart. Slice the cabbage into very thin slices. Briefly soak all the

cabbage slices in a large bowl of water and swish around to clean. Drain.

3. Add the Blackberry Vinegar, ½ cup water, honey, orange zest, dried cranberries, bay leaf, and salt and pepper to the onions and spices in the kettle. Add the cabbage and carefully rotate and toss to make sure all the ingredients are combined. (The cabbage will reduce in size as it cooks.) Cover and cook over moderate heat 15 to 20 minutes, stirring occasionally. Uncover, reduce the heat, and cook for 1 hour, stirring occasionally. Remove the bay leaf and correct the seasonings.

SERVES 8.

Variations:

Substitute Plum Vinegar or black currant vinegar, which is available commercially, for the Blackberry Vinegar. With either substitution, decrease the amount of honey to ¼ cup.

Shallot Oil

10 shallots, sliced
½ cup plus 1 teaspoon canola oil
  or safflower oil
½ cup extra-virgin olive oil

1. Combine the shallots,
½ cup canola oil, and the
olive oil in a saucepan and
gently heat to a bare
simmer. Remove from heat
and pour into a clean jar, let
cool, cover, and let steep in
the refrigerator for 24 to
48 hours.

2. Line a funnel with a
paper coffee filter and use a
pastry brush to paint the
filter with the remaining
teaspoon of canola oil.
Pour the Shallot Oil into
the filter and let it drip
through the funnel into
another very clean jar or
bottle (this may take some
time). Cover or cork
tightly and label with the
date. Store refrigerated.

Makes about 1 cup.

Roasted-Carrot Purée

Carrots never tasted so good. Serve these with game or a roast.

2 pounds carrots
3 tablespoons Shallot Oil
salt
freshly ground black pepper
½ cup milk
1½ tablespoons unsalted butter, cut into bits

1. Preheat oven to 350°F.

2. Peel and trim the carrots and cut them into thirds. Put
   them in a shallow roasting pan and toss them with 1½ tablespoons of the Shallot Oil and some salt and pepper.
   Cover the roasting pan with aluminum foil and seal tightly.
   Roast for 30 minutes. Remove the foil and roast another
   25 to 30 minutes, until the carrots have absorbed all the
   Shallot Oil and are tender when pierced with a fork.

3. Put the carrots, milk, remaining Shallot Oil, and butter in
   a food processor and process until smooth. Season to taste
   with more salt and pepper.

SERVES 6.

Essential Flavors

White Beans with Rosemary Oil

1 pound dried Great Northern or cannellini beans
1 small onion, peeled
1 small carrot, peeled
bouquet garni (celery leaves, bay leaf, sprig of parsley, sprig of thyme, wrapped in cheesecloth and tied with kitchen string)
1 teaspoon salt
freshly ground white pepper
3 tablespoons Rosemary Oil

1. Wash beans and soak overnight, or cover with cold water, boil for 2 minutes, cover tightly, and let stand for 1 hour. Drain.

2. Preheat oven to 275°F.

3. Place beans in a flameproof casserole, add water to cover by 1 inch, and bury onion, carrot, and bouquet garni in beans. Place on a burner and bring to a simmer, then cover and transfer to oven. Bake for 1 to 1½ hours, or until beans are tender (cooking time depends on age of beans). Do not overcook.

4. Pour off any excess water, remove onion, carrot, and bouquet garni, and gently stir in salt, pepper, and Rosemary Oil. Adjust seasoning.

SERVES 8 TO 10.

Variations:

Substitute Roasted-Garlic Oil or Thyme Oil for the Rosemary Oil.

Rosemary Oil

1 ounce fresh rosemary (about 1 cup leaves), rinsed and dried
1 cup extra-virgin olive oil
1 teaspoon canola oil or safflower oil

1. Strip rosemary leaves from the stalks. Combine the leaves and olive oil in a saucepan and warm gently for 5 to 7 minutes. Remove from heat and process in a food processor or blender for 10 seconds. Pour into a very clean jar, let cool, cover, and let steep in the refrigerator for 24 to 48 hours.

2. Line a funnel with a paper coffee filter and use a pastry brush to paint the filter with the teaspoon of canola oil. Pour the Rosemary Oil into the filter and let it drip through the funnel into another very clean jar or bottle (this may take some time). Cover or cork tightly and label with the date. Store refrigerated.

Makes about 1 cup.

Winter Vegetable Purée with Lime Pink Peppercorn Oil

Carrot, parsnip, and beet combine in a velvety purée, the color of a Tahitian sunset.

1 medium or large beet
1 pound carrots, peeled and cut into 2-inch lengths
2 medium parsnips, peeled and cut into 2-inch pieces
salt
1½ tablespoons Lime Pink Peppercorn Oil
freshly ground pepper

1. Preheat oven to 400°F.

2. Wrap the beet (unpeeled) in aluminum foil, place in a small baking dish, and roast for 1 hour, or until tender when poked through the foil with a fork. Unwrap beet and let cool enough to peel it—the skin will come right off. Cut into several pieces.

3. While the beet is roasting, fill a large saucepan with water, add the carrots, parsnips, and salt. Bring to a boil, reduce heat to medium, and cook until carrots are very tender, up to 30 minutes, depending on thickness and age of carrots. Drain.

4. Place carrots, parsnips, and beet in the bowl of a food processor or blender; add the Lime Pink Peppercorn Oil, salt, and a little pepper and process until very smooth. If not serving immediately, keep purée warm in a 250°F. oven or allow it to cool and reheat it in a saucepan just before serving.

SERVES 4 TO 6.

Variations:

Substitute Ginger Oil for the Lime Pink Peppercorn Oil and add a few gratings of fresh nutmeg. Try this one for Thanksgiving!

Parsley root looks like a small parsnip and comes in bunches—the leaves are parsley, but more bitter than the usual kind. If you've ever seen one and wondered what to do with it, here's a good place to start. Substitute ¼ pound parsley roots for the parsnips and add 2 teaspoons sugar.

Potato Purée with Thyme Oil

Thyme Oil

2 small bunches thyme (about
    1 ounce each), rinsed and dried
1⅓ cups extra-virgin olive oil
1 teaspoon canola oil or safflower
    oil

I. Break up the thyme (no
need to remove the leaves
from the stems) and
"bruise" it by smashing it
with a mallet, rolling pin,
or other heavy object.
Place the thyme in a small
saucepan, cover with the
olive oil, and warm gently
for 6 to 7 minutes. Pour it
into a very clean jar, let
cool, cover, and let steep
in the refrigerator for
48 hours.

2. Line a funnel with a
paper coffee filter and use
a pastry brush to paint the
filter with the teaspoon of
canola oil. Pour the Thyme
Oil into the filter and let it
drip through the funnel into
a very clean jar or bottle
(this will take several
hours). Cover or cork
tightly and label with the
date. Store refrigerated.

Makes just over I cup.

If you don't already have a potato ricer, consider picking one up. They're incredibly inexpensive (usually less than five dollars), and not only do they save a lot of time and potato-mashing muscle, they make the fluffiest mashed potatoes in the world—so fluffy that we call them potato purée. (A food mill also works well, but you can mash them the old-fashioned way.) And an added bonus is that despite the fact that this purée has less fat than most mashed potato recipes, it tastes sumptuously rich!

2 pounds Idaho (russet) potatoes
½ teaspoon salt
1 cup milk
freshly ground white pepper
1 tablespoon plus 1 teaspoon Thyme Oil

1. Peel the potatoes and cut them into thick slices. Cover with cold water, add the ½ teaspoon salt, bring to a boil, and cook about 15 to 20 minutes, until tender when pierced with a sharp knife. Do not overcook.

2. While the potatoes are cooking, heat the milk in a small saucepan until hot. Keep warm on low heat.

3. Drain the potatoes well, put them through a potato ricer or food mill back into the saucepan, and stir in the milk. If you don't have a ricer or food mill, mash the potatoes together with the milk. Add the 1 tablespoon of Thyme Oil and salt and pepper to taste. The purée may be prepared up to this point and kept warm in a 250°F. oven.

4. Just before serving, drizzle the remaining 1 teaspoon of
   Thyme Oil over the potatoes.

SERVES 4.

Variations:

Substitute Curry Oil, Chive Oil, Rosemary Oil, or Basil Oil
for Thyme Oil.

Lemon-Herb Oil

1 lemon
1 ounce fresh thyme
1 cup plus 1 teaspoon canola oil
   or safflower oil

1. With a vegetable peeler, peel the yellow zest from the lemon, making sure to leave the white pith on the fruit. Wash the thyme, then break it up and "bruise" it using a mallet, rolling pin, or other heavy object. Put the thyme in a saucepan with the lemon zest and the cup of oil. Warm gently over low heat for 5 minutes. Pour into a very clean jar, let cool, cover, and let steep in the refrigerator for 24 to 48 hours.

2. Line a funnel with a paper coffee filter and use a pastry brush to paint the filter with the remaining teaspoon of oil. Pour the Lemon-Herb Oil into the filter and let it drip through the funnel into another very clean jar or bottle (this may take some time). Cover or cork tightly and label with the date. Store refrigerated.

Makes about 1 cup.

New Potatoes Roasted with Lemon-Herb Oil and Bay Leaves

These potatoes are unusual, pretty, and delicious. The combination of the Lemon-Herb Oil and the bay leaves is heavenly.

2 to 2½ pounds new potatoes, each about the size of a Ping-Pong ball (about 25 to 30 potatoes)
3 tablespoons Lemon-Herb Oil
salt
freshly ground black pepper
25 to 30 bay leaves

1. Preheat the oven to 350°F.

2. Using a sharp paring knife, make a vertical slit *almost* all the way through each potato, so that the potatoes resemble clams. Put the potatoes in a roasting pan and drizzle the Lemon-Herb Oil onto and into the potatoes, making sure that you get some oil into each slit. Toss with salt and pepper. Finally, slide a bay leaf into each slit.

3. Roast the potatoes for 1 hour, shaking the pan every 15 minutes or so to make sure the potatoes are roasting evenly. Keep the bay leaves in for serving but remove before eating.

SERVES 6.

Potato Thimbles with Orange-Parsley Pesto

Surround an important roast with these unusual and pretty potatoes. If you have any Orange-Parsley Pesto left over after filling the potatoes, try tossing some pasta with it.

2 pounds red new potatoes (about 25 to 30 potatoes)
salt
6 tablespoons Orange-Infused Oil*
freshly ground pepper
½ cup pine nuts, toasted**
1 small bunch parsley (the leaves and 1 inch of stem should
measure about a cup)

1. Fill a large saucepan with cold water. Cut the potatoes in half horizontally. Using a sharp paring knife, slice off the small end of each half, so that the potato will sit on that end without wobbling. Then trim each potato half (you will be peeling it at the same time) so that each is faceted with five or six sides. Trim off any remaining peel on each potato, or if you wish, leave a couple of bits on to add some color and variety. As you finish trimming and peeling each potato, put it in the saucepan of cold water.

2. Add some salt to the water in the saucepan and put the potatoes on to boil. Once the potatoes have reached the boiling point, let them cook for 5 minutes. Drain in a colander and refresh with cold water. (NOTE: The potatoes may be held at this stage for several hours.)

* *Not to be confused with commercially available orange oil.*
** *Toast the pine nuts under the broiler or in a dry sauté pan. Watch them with an eagle eye to make sure they don't burn!*

Orange-Infused Oil

2 oranges
1 cup plus 1 teaspoon canola oil
   or safflower oil

1. Using a vegetable peeler, peel the zest away from the two oranges, making sure to leave the bitter white pith on the orange. Cut the orange zest into thinner strips, put them into a saucepan with the cup of oil, and warm gently for 5 minutes. Remove to a very clean jar, let cool, cover, and let steep in the refrigerator for 24 to 48 hours.

2. Line a funnel with a paper coffee filter and use a pastry brush to paint the filter with the remaining teaspoon of oil. Pour the Orange-Infused Oil into the filter and let it drip through the funnel into another very clean jar or bottle (this may take some time). Cover or cork tightly and label with the date. Store refrigerated.

Makes about 1 cup.

---

3. Preheat the oven to 400°F.

4. Pour 1 tablespoon of the Orange-Infused Oil into a large roasting pan and spread it around to make sure that the entire bottom of the pan is covered with oil. Sprinkle some salt and pepper into the pan.

5. Using the small scooper at the end of a vegetable peeler or a small spoon, gently dig out a shallow indentation in the large end of each potato half, leaving a ⅛-inch rim around the indentation. Now that the potatoes are semicooked, this should be easy to do. Place each potato *indentation side down* in the roasting pan. Sprinkle with additional salt and pepper and brush all the potatoes with 1 more table-spoon of the Orange-Infused Oil. Put the pan on the bottom rack of the oven or on the oven floor and roast the potatoes for 45 minutes, or until the edge around the indentation of each potato is golden brown.

6. While the potatoes are roasting, make the filling. (This can also be made in advance, but it will darken somewhat with time, so be sure to keep it well covered with plastic wrap.) In a food processor, grind the toasted pine nuts, then add the parsley and pulse several times. Finally, add the 4 remaining tablespoons of Orange-Infused Oil in a stream and process until well combined. Season to taste with salt and pepper.

7. When the potatoes are done, flip them over and put a small mound of the parsley–pine nut mixture in the indentation. Serve warm.

MAKES ENOUGH TO SURROUND A ROAST, OR SERVES 8 AS A SIDE DISH.

Rosemary Potatoes "Sarladaise"

A new twist on a classic from the lovely medieval town of Sarlat in France's Périgord region. A nonstick skillet makes it easy. If you use red potatoes and want something colorful, leave them unpeeled.

3 tablespoons Rosemary Oil
2 pounds Yukon Gold, Long Island, or red potatoes, peeled
    and cut into ½-inch dice (about 4 large potatoes)
2 cloves garlic, minced
salt
freshly ground black pepper

1. Heat 2 tablespoons of the Rosemary Oil in a nonstick skillet. Add the potatoes, stir with a wooden spoon to coat with the oil, and sauté for 2 minutes. Add the garlic and 1 teaspoon salt, toss to combine, and cover. Turn heat to low and let the potatoes steam for 30 minutes.

2. Remove the cover, turn up the heat to medium, and leave without stirring for 3 to 5 minutes to let the potatoes on the bottom brown. Using a plastic spatula, lift the potatoes and flip them, bringing the browned ones to the top. Leave to brown again. Continue this process at intervals for about another 30 minutes, until all the potatoes are nice and crusty-brown. Halfway through, add pepper and, if necessary, more salt. (NOTE: The potatoes may be prepared to this point, left on top of the stove for up to 1 hour, and reheated briefly.) Drizzle remaining 1 tablespoon of Rosemary Oil over them just before serving.

SERVES 4 TO 6.

Rosemary Oil

1 ounce fresh rosemary (about
    1 cup leaves), rinsed and dried
1 cup extra-virgin olive oil
1 teaspoon canola oil or safflower
    oil

1. Strip rosemary leaves from the stalks. Combine the leaves and olive oil in a saucepan and warm gently for 5 to 7 minutes. Remove from heat and process in a food processor or blender for 10 seconds. Pour into a very clean jar, let cool, cover, and let steep in the refrigerator for 24 to 48 hours.

2. Line a funnel with a paper coffee filter and use a pastry brush to paint the filter with the teaspoon of canola oil. Pour the Rosemary Oil into the filter and let it drip through the funnel into another very clean jar or bottle (this may take some time). Cover or cork tightly and label with the date. Store refrigerated.

Makes about 1 cup.

3 tablespoons cumin seeds or
   3 tablespoons packaged ground
   cumin
1 cup plus 1 teaspoon canola oil
   or safflower oil

1. If you are using cumin seeds, roast them over moderate heat in a dry sauté pan for 2 to 3 minutes, grind them in a spice grinder or mini-chop or with a mortar and pestle, and then combine with the cup of oil and gently warm for 5 minutes.

or

If you are using packaged ground cumin, measure the cumin into a dry, heavy-bottomed saucepan. Gently roast the ground cumin for about 2 minutes over medium heat to release its aroma, then add the cup of oil and gently warm for 5 minutes.

2. Pour into a very clean jar, let cool, cover, and let steep in the refrigerator for 24 to 48 hours. Line a funnel with a paper coffee filter and use a pastry brush to paint the filter with the remaining teaspoon of oil. Pour the Cumin Oil into the filter and let it drip through the funnel into

Roasted Potatoes and Shallots with Cumin Oil

New potatoes work best with this recipe, but quartered or halved Red Bliss or regular boiling potatoes come out beautifully roasted this way, too.

2 pounds potatoes
1 tablespoon extra-virgin olive oil or Shallot Oil
2 tablespoons Cumin Oil
salt
freshly ground black pepper
10 to 12 shallots
1 tablespoon red wine vinegar or Bouquet de Provence Red
    Wine Vinegar (page 53)
1 teaspoon Dijon mustard

1. Preheat the oven to 350°F.

2. Put the potatoes in a roasting pan and toss with the olive oil, 1 tablespoon of the Cumin Oil, salt, and pepper. Roast the potatoes in the oven for 15 minutes, shaking the pan occasionally to make sure the potatoes are roasting evenly.

3. While the potatoes are roasting, peel the papery skin off the shallots, split any double cloves that appear, and chop off the root ends from each clove. After the 15 minutes are up, add the shallots to the potatoes, shaking the pan gently to make sure the shallots are glossed with oil. Return the pan to the oven for an additional 40 to 45 minutes.

4. Whisk together the vinegar, Dijon mustard, salt, and pepper and add the remaining 1 tablespoon of Cumin Oil, a

drop at a time. Remove the pan from the oven and let the potatoes and shallots cool slightly in the pan. Pour the vinaigrette over the potatoes and toss lightly, incorporating whatever oil and browned bits are on the bottom of the pan. Remove all to a serving bowl. Serve slightly warm or at room temperature.

SERVES 4.

another very clean jar or bottle (this may take some time). Cover or cork tightly and label with the date. Store refrigerated.

Makes about 1 cup.

Ginger Oil

*one 4-inch piece ginger root, peeled
and chopped into
small dice*
*1 cup plus 1 teaspoon canola oil
or safflower oil*

1. Combine the ginger and the cup of oil in a saucepan and warm gently for 10 to 12 minutes. Pour into a very clean jar, let cool, cover, and let steep in the refrigerator for 24 to 48 hours.

2. Line a funnel with a paper coffee filter and use a pastry brush to paint the filter with the remaining teaspoon of oil. Pour the Ginger Oil into the filter and let it drip through the funnel into another very clean jar or bottle (this may take some time). Cover or cork tightly and label with the date. Store refrigerated.

Makes about 1 cup.

Lime Ginger Couscous

1 teaspoon salt
1 cup couscous (the instant variety, available in supermarkets)
2 tablespoons finely chopped cilantro
1½ tablespoons fresh lime juice
salt
freshly ground black pepper
¼ cup Ginger Oil
assorted lettuces

1. Bring 1½ cups water to a boil with 1 teaspoon salt in a small saucepan. Add the couscous, cover, remove from the heat, and let sit for 5 minutes.

2. Meanwhile, combine the cilantro, lime juice, salt, and freshly ground pepper. Whisk in the Ginger Oil a drop at a time. When the couscous is done, quickly fluff it with a fork while pouring on the vinaigrette. Serve warm or at room temperature on a bed of assorted lettuces.

SERVES 4.

Couscous with Currants, Scallions, and Opal Basil Vinaigrette

A marvelous accompaniment to leg of lamb.

1 teaspoon salt

1 cup couscous (the instant variety, available in supermarkets)

4 scallions, sliced on the diagonal, including 2 inches of the green part

¼ cup dried currants or raisins

2 tablespoons Opal Basil Vinegar

salt

freshly ground black pepper

¼ cup extra-virgin olive oil

1. Bring 1½ cups water to a boil with 1 teaspoon salt in a small saucepan. Stir in the couscous, scallions, and currants, remove from the heat, and cover the pan. Let stand for 5 minutes.

2. While the couscous is standing, make the vinaigrette: In a small bowl, combine the Opal Basil Vinegar, salt, and pepper. Whisk in the olive oil, drop by drop, until all is incorporated. When the couscous is done, quickly fluff it with a fork, transfer to a serving bowl, pour on the vinaigrette, and toss to combine.

SERVES 4.

Variations:

Substitute Sage Vinegar or Pink Tarragon Vinegar for the Opal Basil Vinegar.

Opal Basil Vinegar

1 bundle fresh opal (purple) basil leaves (about 1 ounce)
2 cups white wine vinegar

1. Rinse the basil and discard any blackened leaves. Put all the basil into a very clean jar. Heat the vinegar until warm to the touch but not hot, pour it over the herbs, and swirl it around to make sure the herbs are covered. Let cool, cover, label with the date, and let stand in a cool, dark place for 10 to 14 days.

2. Strain through a cheesecloth-lined funnel into a very clean jar or bottle; cover or cork tightly. Keep in a cool, dark place.

Makes about 2 cups.

Wild and Basmati Rice with Leek Elixir

Leek Elixir

green parts of 6 to 8 leeks
1 cup dry white wine
3 tablespoons fresh thyme or
*   1½ tablespoons dried*
2 tablespoons black peppercorns
1 teaspoon salt

1. Wash the leek tops, rinsing them thoroughly in at least three or four changes of water to make sure you get rid of all the grit that tends to be lodged between the leaves. Chop them into 1-inch strips. You should have about 8 cups, packed.

2. Combine all ingredients with 6 cups water in a large kettle or stockpot. Bring the water to a boil, reduce the heat, and simmer, partially covered, for 25 minutes. Remove from the heat and let stand 10 minutes.

3. Pour the Leek Elixir through a strainer into a very clean container and let cool. Cover and store refrigerated. Leek Elixir may also be frozen.

Makes about 6 cups.

2 cups Leek Elixir
½ cup wild rice
½ cup basmati rice
salt

1. Bring Leek Elixir to a boil in a saucepan with a tight-fitting cover. Add wild rice, stir briefly, cover, and turn heat to low. Cook for 25 minutes.

2. Add basmati rice (if using Indian or bulk basmati, rinse the rice first), stir to combine, cover, and continue cooking for another 15 minutes. Add salt to taste, fluff with a fork, and serve immediately.

SERVES 4.

Rice Pilaf with Cumin Oil
and Cilantro

Our favorite way to cook rice is to bake it—happily, a method that leaves lots of room for experimentation. Here is the result of a successful experiment.

2 tablespoons Cumin Oil
2 tablespoons minced shallots
1 cup white rice
1 cup beef or chicken stock, homemade or canned
¼ teaspoon Tabasco
salt
freshly ground black pepper
1 tablespoon finely chopped cilantro

1. Preheat the oven to 350°F.

2. In an ovenproof saucepan with a tight-fitting lid, warm the Cumin Oil gently with the shallots (it shouldn't get too hot). Add the rice and swirl it around until all the grains are covered with the oil. Add 1 cup water, the stock, Tabasco, salt, and pepper and bring to a boil. Reduce heat and simmer for 1 minute. Cover, place in the oven, and bake for 30 minutes. Remove the lid and bake for an additional 10 minutes.

3. Remove from the oven and fluff with a fork. Toss in the cilantro leaves. Correct seasoning if necessary.

SERVES 4.

Cumin Oil

3 tablespoons cumin seeds or
*   3 tablespoons packaged ground*
*   cumin*
1 cup plus 1 teaspoon canola oil
*   or safflower oil*

1. If using cumin seeds, roast them over moderate heat in a dry sauté pan 2 to 3 minutes, grind in a spice grinder or mini-chop or use a mortar and pestle, and combine with the cup of oil and gently warm 5 minutes.
   or
If you are using packaged ground cumin, measure the cumin into a dry, heavy-bottomed saucepan. Gently roast the ground cumin for about 2 minutes over medium heat to release its aroma, then add the cup of oil and gently warm for 5 minutes.

2. Pour into a very clean jar, let cool, cover, and let steep in the refrigerator for 24 to 48 hours. Line a funnel with a paper coffee filter and use a pastry brush to paint the filter with the remaining teaspoon of oil. Pour the Cumin Oil into the filter and let it drip through the funnel into another very clean jar or bottle. Cover or cork tightly and label with the date. Store refrigerated.

Makes about 1 cup.

Rosemary-Oil Olive Country Bread

This makes an informal but flavorful focaccia-like bread. Knead the dough by hand, in a food processor, or in an electric mixer with a dough hook.

1 package active dry yeast
¾ cup warm water (105° to 110°F.)
pinch of unbleached all-purpose flour
pinch of sugar
2 cups unbleached all-purpose flour, plus some extra for kneading
½ cup rye flour
1 teaspoon salt
2 tablespoons Rosemary Oil, plus extra for brushing the top of the bread before baking
dash of safflower oil
2 tablespoons chopped fresh rosemary (optional)
8 to 10 large black cured olives (not canned), such as kalamata, pitted and cut into slices
handful of cornmeal
¼ cup coarsely grated Parmesan cheese (optional)

1. To proof the yeast, mix the yeast with the water, pinch of flour, and pinch of sugar. Let stand 5 to 10 minutes, until it begins to get foamy (thus "proving" that it is alive).

2. Mix together the all-purpose and rye flours and the salt. Add the yeast-water mixture and Rosemary Oil to the flours and stir until well blended. If the dough is gooey, add a bit more flour; if it is too hard or crumbly, add more

water 1 teaspoon at a time. Knead for an additional 5 minutes, either on a clean, lightly floured surface by hand, in the food processor (2 to 3 minutes should do it), or in a mixer with a dough hook, varying the speed as needed. Knead the dough until it is smooth and firm. It may still be mildly sticky.

3. Oil a large bowl with the safflower oil, transfer the dough to it, cover with a clean kitchen cloth, and allow to rest in a warm place until it doubles in size, about 1 hour. (If it doesn't start to grow in the first 30 minutes, return to step 1 and start over again—and consider buying a new batch of yeast.) Punch the dough down and work in the chopped rosemary, if using, and the olive slices. Let the dough rest for a few minutes.

4. Sprinkle cornmeal on the bottom of a 9-inch or 10-inch springform pan. Lightly flour your hands, pat the dough into some semblance of a circle, and put it in the pan. Stretch and prod the dough outward in all directions until it covers the bottom of the pan. Cover with a clean kitchen cloth and let rise again for 30 minutes.

5. Preheat the oven to 450°F.

6. Just before popping the bread into the oven, brush the dough with additional Rosemary Oil and sprinkle on the Parmesan cheese, if using. Bake the bread for 10 to 15 minutes, or until it is browned and sounds hollow when tapped. Remove pan from oven and let bread cool on a rack.

MAKES 8 WEDGES AND SERVES 2, 4, OR 8, DEPENDING ON THE REST OF YOUR MENU.

CHAPTER NINE

Desserts

A nd finally, a sweet ending. Although we know of people who profess not to like sweets, it always turns out that there is one special dessert they will gobble down greedily. Other people quite frankly acknowledge their sweet tooth. "What's for dessert?" they'll ask, with the sweet look of childhood innocence on their smiling faces.

A wise hostess once suggested to us that it didn't really matter what else was served at a dinner party, as long as the dessert was a winner. Here is our collection of those essential, winning desserts, for dining-room dinner parties or casual suppers at home in the kitchen.

Peaches Poached in Port-Pepper-Sage Elixir

These remind us of jeweled fruit in the hanging gardens of Babylon.

2 cups Port-Pepper-Sage Elixir
¼ cup sugar
6 ripe peaches
6 sage leaves

1. In a saucepan large enough to accommodate all the peaches, combine the Port-Pepper-Sage Elixir with the sugar over medium heat and cook until the sugar dissolves.

2. Add the peaches, with their skins on, and poach them gently for 10 minutes. If the liquid comes only halfway up the sides of the peaches, turn them after 5 minutes so that they will be evenly poached.

3. Remove the peaches from the poaching liquid and peel them—their skins should come off easily, leaving you with lovely jewel-like fruits. Arrange the peaches in a serving dish (slice a tiny bit off their bottoms if necessary to help them stand up straight) and place a sage leaf on top of each peach, to look as if it is attached to the peach stem.

4. Reduce the poaching liquid over moderately high heat until it is syrupy—you should have about 1 cup. Pour the syrup in a lake around the peaches.

SERVES 6.

Port-Pepper-Sage Elixir

3 cups ruby port
1 bunch fresh sage, finely chopped
(about 1 ounce)
3 to 4 grindings of black pepper

1. Combine the ingredients in a saucepan and bring to a boil. Reduce heat and simmer, uncovered, 20 to 25 minutes, until the elixir has been reduced to 2 cups.

2. Strain into a very clean bottle, let cool, cover, and label. Store refrigerated.

Makes 2 cups.

Essential Flavors

Pear Fans Baked in Vanilla-Rum Elixir

Serve these beautiful, flavorful pears with almond tuiles or plain, crisp butter cookies.

1 teaspoon unsalted butter
3 tablespoons raisins
3 ripe Bartlett or Bosc pears
1 to 2 teaspoons fresh lemon juice
3 tablespoons sugar
½ cup Vanilla-Rum Elixir
2 tablespoons heavy cream

1. Find a shallow baking dish large enough to hold 6 pear halves. Grease the inside of the baking dish with the butter.

2. Preheat the oven to 350°F.

3. Combine the raisins and ½ cup water in a small saucepan and bring to a simmer over gentle heat. Remove and let stand for 20 minutes.

4. To prevent discoloration, work on one pear at a time. Halve the pears, leaving the stems intact where possible. Peel and use a small spoon or melon baller to remove the seeds. Put the pear on your work surface, cut side down, with the narrow end farthest away from you. Keeping in mind that you want to keep the narrow end intact, make four or five vertical cuts down each pear, starting 1 inch from the top, or narrow end, and going all the way to the bottom.

Vanilla-Rum Elixir

2 cups golden rum, such as Mount Gay
4 vanilla beans

1. Pour the rum into a very clean jar. Split the vanilla beans lengthwise, scrape out the seeds in the center, and add the seeds to the rum. Cut the vanilla beans into 1-inch pieces and add to the rum. Let steep, covered, for 5 to 7 days.

2. Strain out the amount of elixir you need as you use it. Add replacement rum to the jar so that you always have some elixir on hand, steeping. You do not need to replace the vanilla beans each time, but you might want to add a new bean every other time you deplete your whole jar of elixir.

Makes 2 cups.

---

5. As you finish each pear half, put it in the baking dish, cut side down, and brush it with lemon juice. When all the pears are in the baking dish, sprinkle the sugar over them and then pour the Vanilla-Rum Elixir over all. It should come about one-third of the way up the sides of the pears. Pour the raisins and their liquid over all. (NOTE: You can hold the pears this way for about 1 hour, but after that they may start to discolor.)

6. Bake the pears for 30 minutes, basting once. They will fan out as they bake. Remove the pan from the oven and, using a spatula, move the pears to a platter, arranging them with their narrow ends toward the middle. Use a fork to help separate or fan out any recalcitrant pears.

7. Set the pears aside, loosely covered with foil, until ready to serve, and pour the sauce into a small saucepan. Just before serving, add 1 tablespoon water to the sauce, bring to a bare simmer, and whisk in the cream. Pour it over the pears.

SERVES 4 TO 6.

Gingery Apple Pie

Granny Smith apples give this pie a lively tartness; Ginger Oil provides the counterpoint. If you prefer a sweeter pie, use half Granny Smith and half Golden Delicious.

For the crust:
1½ cups unbleached all-purpose flour

1 teaspoon salt

1 stick cold unsalted butter, cut into bits

1 egg, lightly beaten

1 tablespoon milk

3 tablespoons ice water

For the filling:
6 Granny Smith apples (or 3 Granny Smith and 3 Golden
    Delicious), peeled, cored, quartered, and thinly sliced

1 tablespoon fresh lemon juice

1½ tablespoons Ginger Oil, plus a little extra for greasing
    the pie plate

4 tablespoons brown sugar

1 tablespoon unbleached all-purpose flour

⅛ teaspoon freshly grated nutmeg

¼ teaspoon cinnamon

For the top:
1 tablespoon cream (light or heavy)

2 teaspoons sugar

1. To make the crust: In the bowl of a food processor, combine flour and salt; process briefly to combine. Add the
bits of cold butter and process until mixture resembles

Ginger Oil

*one 4-inch piece ginger root, peeled
   and chopped into
   small dice*

*1 cup plus 1 teaspoon canola oil
   or safflower oil*

1. Combine the ginger and
the cup of oil in a saucepan
and warm gently for 10 to
12 minutes. Pour into a
very clean jar, let cool,
cover, and let steep in the
refrigerator for 24 to
48 hours.

2. Line a funnel with a
paper coffee filter and use
a pastry brush to paint the
filter with the remaining
teaspoon of oil. Pour the
Ginger Oil into the filter
and let it drip through the
funnel into another very
clean jar or bottle (this may
take some time). Cover or
cork tightly and label with
the date. Store refrigerated.

Makes about 1 cup.

coarse meal, about 10 seconds. Add the egg, milk, and ice water; process until the dough forms a ball. Divide equally and flatten dough slightly into two disc shapes, wrap in a cloth, and chill in the refrigerator for 1 to 2 hours.

2. Preheat oven to 350°F.

3. To make the filling: Sprinkle the apple slices with the lemon juice as soon as they are sliced to prevent discoloration, then toss with the Ginger Oil. In a small bowl, combine 3 tablespoons of the brown sugar, the 1 tablespoon flour, the nutmeg, and the cinnamon. Add to the apples and toss to coat.

4. Grease a 9½-inch (measurement across top) glass pie plate or pie tin with a little Ginger Oil. On a lightly floured board, roll out half of the dough into a 14-inch circle about ⅛ inch thick. Fold the circle in quarters, place it in the pie plate, unfold, and fit it into the plate. Pour in the apples, which will be generously heaped. Sprinkle the remaining 1 tablespoon of brown sugar over them.

5. Roll out the remaining half of the dough into a 14-inch circle, fold it in quarters, lay it over the pie, and unfold it. Trim dough if necessary to yield a 1½-inch overhang. Fold the overhang under, leaving a thick ½-inch overhang, and crimp edges. Using a small sharp knife, cut five 2-inch vents radiating outward from the center. Brush the top of the crust with the cream and sprinkle with the granulated sugar.

6. Bake for 45 to 50 minutes, or until the crust is golden brown. Let cool 1 hour or so before serving.

SERVES 6.

Essential Flavors

Lindsay Torte, or Fig Essence and Pistachio Tart

A magnificent combination of our favorite flavors from the Mediterranean, named after a friend of ours who is wild about figs but hates to make pastry.

For the crust:
1 pound salted undyed pistachios
1 cup unbleached all-purpose flour
⅓ cup sugar
6 tablespoons cold unsalted butter, cut into bits
2 tablespoons walnut oil

For the filling:
¾ cup Fig Essence
12 to 14 fresh small black mission figs
1 teaspoon sugar

1. Preheat the oven to 425°F.

2. Find an 8-inch tart pan with a removable bottom.

3. Shell the pistachios until you have ¾ cup shelled pistachios. You should have more than enough if you start with 1 pound, but you can use the extra to tempt people into the kitchen to help you with the task.

4. In a food processor, grind the pistachios until they are the texture of coarse sand. Add the flour and sugar and process until blended. Add the butter bits and pulse 5 times. Then, with the processor on, pour 2 to 3 table-

Fig Essence

1 pound fresh small black mission figs
2 tablespoons dry white wine
2 tablespoons fresh lemon juice
1 teaspoon vanilla extract or Vanilla-Rum Elixir (page 80)
1 tablespoon sugar
two 1-inch-long strips of lemon zest

I. Wash the figs and chop them coarsely. Combine all ingredients in a saucepan and cook, covered, over medium heat for 10 to 15 minutes, stirring every 4 to 5 minutes.

2. Pour the contents of the saucepan into a food mill or sieve placed over a large bowl. Force the Fig Essence through the food mill or sieve until all that remains behind are the fig skins, lemon zest, and a bit of fig pulp, which you can discard. The Fig Essence in the bowl should be almost jamlike in consistency. Transfer to a clean container and refrigerate for later use or use immediately.

Makes about I cup.

spoons cold water and the walnut oil through the feed tube and process until the pastry forms a ball.

5. Remove the pastry from the food processor and pat it into the tart pan, making sure that you have even coverage everywhere. The back of a spoon helps to smooth out the rough spots. Place a piece of kitchen parchment paper (foil works, too, but it may stick to the pastry) on top of the pastry shell and pour on some pie weights (several cups of dispensable beans have always worked for us) to keep the pastry from bubbling up while it's baking. Bake for 15 minutes. Remove from the oven and remove the parchment paper and weights. Return to the oven for an additional 10 minutes, until the edges look browned and the bottom has lost its shiny look.

6. Remove the crust from the oven, reduce the heat to 350°F., and pour the Fig Essence into the tart shell. Remove the stems from the fresh figs, quarter them lengthwise, and place them, seed side up, in concentric circles on top of the Fig Essence. The cut figs should fill the entire top of the tart. Sprinkle lightly with the sugar. If the edge of the crust is very brown (which is quite possible), cover it with aluminum foil to prevent it from burning. Return tart to the oven and bake for 35 minutes. Cool and remove the side ring from the tart.

SERVES 6 TO 8.

Hazelnut Ginger Pear
Tarte "Tatin"

There are two ways to make the nut-rich crust for this upside-down tart—if Method I doesn't seem to be working, you can easily move on to Method II. Since the tart is flipped, you're the only one who needs to know what the bottom looks like.

The combination of pears, hazelnuts, and Ginger Oil is irresistible—and worth a crack at the crust. This tart goes very well with vanilla ice cream or a dollop of homemade crème fraîche (see page 254).

For the crust:
2½ cups shelled hazelnuts

⅓ cup dark brown sugar, packed

1½ cups unbleached all-purpose flour

pinch of salt

6 tablespoons cold unsalted butter, cut into bits

3 tablespoons hazelnut oil or walnut oil

3 tablespoons ice water

For the bottom that ends up as the top:
¼ cup dark brown sugar, packed

¼ cup sugar

3 tablespoons Ginger Oil

2 tablespoons fresh lemon juice

6 ripe Bosc pears

1. To toast the hazelnuts, put them in a cake pan or roasting pan and put the pan in a cold oven. Turn the oven up to 350°F. and heat the nuts for 25 minutes (set a timer so that you won't overbake and waste a batch). Remove the nuts from the oven and let them cool. When they are cool

---

Ginger Oil

one 4-inch piece ginger root, peeled
  and chopped into
  small dice
1 cup plus 1 teaspoon canola oil
  or safflower oil

I. Combine the ginger and the cup of oil in a saucepan and warm gently for 10 to 12 minutes. Pour into a very clean jar, let cool, cover, and let steep in the refrigerator for 24 to 48 hours.

2. Line a funnel with a paper coffee filter and use a pastry brush to paint the filter with the remaining teaspoon of oil. Pour the Ginger Oil into the filter and let it drip through the funnel into another very clean jar or bottle (this may take some time). Cover or cork tightly and label with the date. Store refrigerated.

Makes about 1 cup.

enough to handle, rub them together between your hands or in a clean kitchen cloth to remove the brown, papery skins (not all the skins will come off). Select 1⅓ cups' worth of skinned or mostly skinned nuts. (The rest are good for snacking or staving off hungry kitchen interlopers.)

2. Briefly grind the nuts in a food processor. Add the brown sugar, flour, and salt and pulse several times until combined. Add the butter bits and pulse 15 times. With the food processor on, add the hazelnut oil and ice water and process until the dough begins to form a ball. Turn the dough out onto a clean surface and briefly massage it until it holds together and is somewhat uniform-looking. Flatten into a disc, wrap in plastic, and refrigerate for 1 hour.

3. Preheat the oven to 375°F.

4. In the bottom of a 9½-inch (top measurement) Pyrex pie dish, combine the brown and white sugars. Add the Ginger Oil and lemon juice and mix with a fork until a caramel-colored liquid paste covers the bottom of the pie pan.

5. Pick up your first pear and cut it in half vertically. Take one of the halves and, using a melon baller or small spoon, scoop out the core and the stem. Peel. Chop off the top and bottom ends of the pear half and reserve. Cut the pear half into thin horizontal slices, keeping it together as you slice. Place the pear half, cored side up, in the baking dish, with the top end pointing toward the center of the dish. Repeat with the other pear half and 3 of the remaining pears, placing them side by side in the baking dish like spokes in a wheel. (Depending on the size of your pears, you may be able to fit only 7 halves, or 3½ pears, into the

pan this way.) Put a final pear half in the center, also cored side up. Peel and chop up the remaining pears and scatter them and the reserved top and bottom pieces on top of the pears in the pan.

6. Retrieve the dough and place it between two sheets of wax paper or kitchen parchment paper, and try one of these two approaches to the dough:

Method I: With a rolling pin, roll out the dough between the sheets of paper into a circle about 12 inches in diameter. Remove the top piece of paper and slide your hands underneath the bottom piece of paper. Lift up the dough, while it is still on the paper, and flip it over onto the pears in the baking dish. Peel away the paper and tuck the extra dough down into the side of the pan. Patch any holes with pinches of dough from areas where the crust is thickest.

Method II: With a rolling pin, roll out the dough between the sheets of paper into a rectangle approximately 16 inches x 13 inches. Peel up large sections of the dough and place them in a patchwork over the pears, covering the entire dish, making sure to tuck the dough down the sides of the dish. Use leftover small pieces to patch any holes.

Put the dish on a baking sheet and bake for 1 hour.

7. Remove from the oven and cool for 30 minutes. Run a knife around the edges and then place a serving dish over the glass pie dish and flip the tart. It should come right out.

SERVES 8.

Peppermint Elixir

3 tablespoons dried peppermint
(available in spice shops, or
substitute 4 bags of peppermint
herb tea)
2 cups boiling water

1. Place peppermint in a
teapot or heatproof pitcher
or bowl. Let water stand for
about 10 seconds (it should
be just off boiling), then
pour over the peppermint.
Let steep 8 to 10 minutes.
Do not let it steep too long
or it will turn bitter.

2. Strain into a very clean
jar, cover and store in the
refrigerator.

Makes 1½ cups.

This smooth, deep, dark confection defines what chocolate is all about; the Peppermint Elixir adds the harmonious essential undertone. Use the finest bittersweet chocolate you can find—Lindt Excellence is our favorite.

6 ounces finest-quality bittersweet chocolate
1 cup Peppermint Elixir
6 egg yolks
whipped cream (optional)
sprigs of mint, for garnish

1. Break up the chocolate into pieces in a heavy-bottomed saucepan, pour in Peppermint Elixir to cover, and melt over low heat. When chocolate starts to melt, stir it with a wooden spoon, watching it like a hawk so it doesn't burn. Continue stirring until chocolate is completely melted, combined with elixir, and smooth and glossy. With heat still very low, stir in the egg yolks all at once. Stirring constantly, cook the mixture until it's thickened and very smooth (or reads 180°F. on an instant-read thermometer, if you have one). It may take a while (up to 20 minutes), but resist the temptation to turn up the heat, or the eggs may coagulate.

2. When the mixture is thick, remove from heat and continue stirring for 3 to 4 minutes as it cools. Pour through a strainer into four 4-ounce ramekins. Chill until set.

3. To serve, garnish each pot de crème with a dollop of whipped cream, if desired, and a pretty sprig of mint.

SERVES 4.

Dried-Fruit Crumble with Vanilla-Rum Elixir and Coconut

1 cup dried apricots

½ cup pitted prunes

¼ cup dried cherries or dried cranberries

¼ cup raisins

¼ cup Vanilla-Rum Elixir

¼ cup sugar

For the topping:

⅓ cup unsweetened coconut

¼ cup rolled oats

¼ cup dark brown sugar, packed

⅓ cup unbleached all-purpose flour

5 tablespoons cold unsalted butter, cut into bits

crème fraîche (see page 254) or heavy cream

1. Place the dried apricots, prunes, dried cherries, and raisins in a saucepan with 3 cups water. Bring to a boil, turn down the heat to low, and simmer for 45 minutes. Pour all into a shallow baking dish and let cool slightly. Some of the apricots will have come apart into 2 halves—if any remain whole, pull them apart into 2 halves. Stir in the Vanilla-Rum Elixir, the ¼ cup sugar, and ½ cup water and combine.

2. Preheat the oven to 350°F.

3. To prepare the crumble topping: Mix together the coconut, oats, brown sugar, and flour. Combine well with your hands or in a food processor. Add the butter and, if

---

Vanilla-Rum Elixir

2 cups golden rum, such as Mount Gay
4 vanilla beans

1. Pour the rum into a very clean jar. Split the vanilla beans lengthwise, scrape out the seeds in the center, and add the seeds to the rum. Cut the vanilla beans into 1-inch pieces and add to the rum. Let steep, covered, for 5 to 7 days.

2. Strain out the amount of elixir you need as you use it. Add replacement rum to the jar so that you always have some elixir on hand, steeping. You do not need to replace the vanilla beans each time, but you might want to add a new bean every other time you deplete your whole jar of elixir.

Makes 2 cups.

*How to Make Your Own
Crème Fraîche*

Crème fraîche may be made
quickly and easily at home,
and it's much less expen-
sive than buying it. Simply
whisk together equal
amounts of sour cream
and heavy cream (not
ultrapasteurized) until
the mixture is thick and
smooth. Cover loosely
with plastic and let stand,
unrefrigerated, overnight.
Transfer the crème fraîche
to a covered container
and store refrigerated.
It's ready to use now but
will continue to improve.
It lasts about I week.

you are working with your hands, rub it into the dry ingredients until it is well blended and the mixture has the
texture of coarse meal, or pulse it about 10 times. There
should be no big lumps of butter. Scatter evenly over the
fruit and put the dish in the oven to bake for 40 to 45
minutes.

4. Remove from the oven and serve with crème fraîche or
heavy cream.

SERVES 6 TO 8.

Orange Bittersweet Chocolate Soufflé

There's nothing in the world better than chocolate soufflé, and this one draws raves!

4 tablespoons plus ½ teaspoon Orange-Infused Oil*
4 tablespoons sugar
2½ tablespoons unbleached all-purpose flour
1 cup milk
12 ounces finest-quality bittersweet chocolate (we recommend four 3-ounce bars Lindt Excellence), broken into pieces
¼ cup fresh orange juice
¼ cup Grand Marnier or other orange liqueur (or an additional ¼ cup fresh orange juice)
4 egg yolks
6 egg whites
homemade crème fraîche (page 254), store-bought crème fraîche, or freshly whipped cream flavored with orange liqueur

**Not to be confused with commercially available orange oil.*

1. Locate an 8-cup soufflé dish. Coat the inside of the dish with the ½ teaspoon Orange-Infused Oil and sprinkle 1 tablespoon of the sugar onto the inside, rolling the dish around to coat all sides with the sugar. The sugar acts as a ladder for the soufflé, helping it to climb up the sides of the dish.

2. Gently heat 3 tablespoons of the Orange-Infused Oil in a heavy-bottomed saucepan and add the flour. Cook over

---

Orange-Infused Oil

2 oranges
1 cup plus 1 teaspoon canola oil or safflower oil

1. Using a vegetable peeler, peel the zest away from the two oranges, making sure to leave the bitter white pith on the orange. Cut the orange zest into thinner strips, put them into a saucepan with the cup of oil, and warm gently for 5 minutes. Remove to a very clean jar, let cool, cover, and let steep in the refrigerator for 24 to 48 hours.

2. Line a funnel with a paper coffee filter and use a pastry brush to paint the filter with the remaining teaspoon of oil. Pour the Orange-Infused Oil into the filter and let it drip through the funnel into another very clean jar or bottle (this may take some time). Cover or cork tightly and label with the date. Store refrigerated.

Makes about 1 cup.

moderate heat until this "roux" begins to bubble, and then cook for 2 more minutes, stirring constantly with a whisk. Add the milk slowly and continue to whisk. Don't be perturbed if the mixture gets all clumped together— just continue to whisk, cooking over moderate heat, until it begins to boil. Boil slowly for 2 minutes, still whisking. The lumps should have smoothed out by now. Remove from the heat and add the chocolate, stirring to incorporate the chocolate as it melts. Stir in the last tablespoon Orange-Infused Oil, the remaining 3 tablespoons sugar, the orange juice, and the Grand Marnier. Stir until the mixture is thick and glossy-looking. Transfer to a large bowl, cover, and set aside until just before you are ready to bake it.

3. Preheat the oven to 375°F.

4. Whisk the 4 egg yolks into the chocolate mixture. Beat the 6 egg whites until they hold stiff peaks. Stir a healthy spoonful of the egg whites into the soufflé base to lighten it. Fold in the remaining egg whites. Pour all into the soufflé dish and bake for 40 minutes. Serve immediately, and pass the crème fraîche or flavored whipped cream.

SERVES 6.

Mint Julep Bread Pudding

It seems that every time you turn around, someone is thinking up a new angle on that time-honored, old-fashioned dessert, bread pudding. We're downright excited about ours.

1 cup Mint Julep Elixir
1 teaspoon unsalted butter
25 to 28 slices French bread, about ½ inch thick
3 eggs
1 cup sugar
1½ cups milk
1 cup heavy cream

1. Put the Mint Julep Elixir in a small saucepan and heat to a lively simmer. Simmer for 10 minutes, or until reduced by half.

2. Smear the butter onto the bottom and sides of a shallow baking dish (approximately 8 inches x 11 inches, or 8½ inches in diameter if you are using a round one). Arrange the bread slices so that they overlap into two long columns if you are using a rectangular dish or in concentric circles if you are using a round dish.

3. With an electric mixer, beat the eggs and sugar together until light and frothy. Add the milk, cream, and reduced Mint Julep Elixir and beat to combine well. Pour this over the bread in the shallow baking dish. The bread may seem to float a bit, but it will eventually soak up the custard and sink down. Place two saucers on top of the bread pudding

Mint Julep Elixir

2 cups fresh peppermint leaves, rinsed and patted dry
2 cups high-quality bourbon, such as Maker's Mark, Jack Daniel's, or Jim Beam

1. Remove any peppermint leaves that are turning black, as they will discolor the elixir. Using a mallet, rolling pin, or other heavy object, "bruise" the green leaves; place them in a very clean mason jar and pour the bourbon over them.

2. Cover the jar tightly and let steep for 24 hours, then strain through a cheesecloth-lined funnel into a very clean bottle or jar. Cover or cork tightly. Refrigeration is unnecessary.

Makes 2 cups.

to weight the bread down, and make sure the top of the bread is covered with liquid. Soak for 45 minutes to 1 hour.

4. Preheat the oven to 350°F.

5. Remove the saucers and bake the bread pudding for 1 hour. The bread should be lightly golden and crusty on the top and should have soaked up all the custard. Remove from the oven, let cool slightly, and serve.

SERVES 6.

Mint-Infused Blackberry Ice

Don't let anyone into the kitchen while you're making this, otherwise it'll never make it to the freezer. We ourselves have been known to drink this instead of freezing it! In fact, this dessert alone is reason enough to pick up an ice-cream maker—try one of the handy freezer models.

½ cup sugar
1¼ cups Peppermint Elixir
12 ounces fresh blackberries

1. Dissolve sugar in 1 cup of the Peppermint Elixir, bring to a simmer, and continue simmering for 3 minutes.

2. Pour the blackberries into the bowl of a food processor or blender, add the remaining ¼ cup Peppermint Elixir, and purée. Using a spatula, force purée through a strainer to remove seeds. Don't forget to scrape the thick juice off the bottom of the strainer.

3. Add the sweetened Peppermint Elixir to the purée, chill thoroughly, and freeze in an ice-cream maker according to manufacturer's directions.

MAKES ABOUT 1 PINT, ENOUGH FOR 4 SERVINGS (OR 2 SERVINGS IF YOU LIKE THIS AS MUCH AS WE DO!).

Peppermint Elixir

3 tablespoons dried peppermint (available in spice shops, or substitute 4 bags of peppermint herb tea)
2 cups boiling water

1. Place peppermint in a teapot or heatproof pitcher or bowl. Let water stand for about 10 seconds (it should be just off boiling), then pour over the peppermint. Let steep 8 to 10 minutes. Do not let it steep too long, or it will turn bitter.

2. Strain into a very clean jar, cover, and store in the refrigerator.

Makes 1½ cups.

Plum Elixir Ice Cream

Plum Elixir

½ cup dry white wine
⅓ cup Madeira or dry sherry
1 cup dark brown sugar, packed
one 2-inch piece fresh ginger root,
    peeled and thinly sliced
1 tablespoon black peppercorns
juice and peel of 1 orange
juice and peel of 2 lemons
3 star anise or 1 teaspoon fennel
    seeds
10 plums, rinsed

1. In a stockpot, combine all ingredients except the plums with 5 cups water. Bring to a boil, stirring occasionally. Reduce heat and simmer for 10 minutes.

2. Cut an X at the bottom of each plum and add the plums to the poaching liquid. Poach 10 to 15 minutes, or until the skins start to loosen. With a slotted spoon, remove each plum, dunk it briefly in a bowl of ice water, and remove the skin. Reserve plums for another use. Return skins to the poaching liquid.

3. Continue simmering the poaching liquid for another 15 minutes; strain the liquid and discard the solids. Return the liquid to a saucepan and reduce until you have 2 cups Plum Elixir.

Makes 2 cups.

Homemade ice cream is easier to make than you think. All you need is an ice-cream maker and a recipe like this—or the two that follow—to tempt you along!

2 cups heavy cream
2 cups milk
1 vanilla bean
6 egg yolks
½ cup sugar
¾ cup Plum Elixir

1. Pour the cream and milk into a large saucepan, cut open the vanilla bean lengthwise, and scrape the insides into the saucepan; then drop in the whole pod. Scald the mixture, then cover and let the vanilla infuse for 30 minutes.

2. Set a sieve lined with a layer of cheesecloth over a large bowl or pitcher. Keep handy.

3. Using an electric mixer, beat the egg yolks and sugar until thick and pale yellow.

4. Add Plum Elixir to cream mixture and heat to scalding again. Whisk about one-fourth of the cream mixture into the egg yolks, then pour all the egg yolk mixture back into the saucepan with the cream mixture. Stirring constantly with a wooden spoon, cook over low heat until the custard is thick enough to coat the back of the spoon or reads 180°F. on an instant-read thermometer. (Don't stop stir-

ring or cook over too high a heat or the egg yolks may curdle.) This process takes about 20 minutes.

5. When the custard is thick, pour immediately through the cheesecloth-lined sieve into the bowl or pitcher, stir a few times to bring down the temperature, and chill well. Freeze in an ice-cream maker according to manufacturer's directions. When the ice cream is frozen, pack it into a freezer container and freeze 2 to 8 hours for its final "set" before serving.

MAKES ABOUT 1 QUART.

Fig Essence Ice Cream

Fig Essence

1 pound fresh small black mission figs
2 tablespoons dry white wine
2 tablespoons fresh lemon juice
1 teaspoon vanilla extract or Vanilla-Rum Elixir (page 80)
1 tablespoon sugar
two 1-inch-long strips of lemon zest

I. Wash the figs and chop them coarsely. Combine all ingredients in a saucepan and cook, covered, over medium heat for 10 to 15 minutes, stirring every 4 to 5 minutes.

2. Pour the contents of the saucepan into a food mill or sieve placed over a large bowl. Force the Fig Essence through the food mill or sieve until all that remains behind are the fig skins and lemon zest and a bit of fig pulp, which you can discard. The Fig Essence in the bowl should be almost jamlike in consistency. Transfer to a clean container and refrigerate for later use or use immediately.

Makes about 1 cup.

1 cup Fig Essence
3 tablespoons port
1 cup cream
2 cups milk
1 cup sugar
4 egg yolks

1. Combine the Fig Essence and port and simmer for 10 minutes. Let cool.

2. Line a sieve with cheesecloth and place it over a large bowl or pitcher.

3. Combine the cream and milk and scald in a heavy-bottomed saucepan. Remove from heat.

4. With an electric mixer, combine the sugar and egg yolks and beat until thick and pale yellow—about 2 to 3 minutes.

5. Pour one-third of the warm milk-cream mixture into the egg mixture, whisking well to combine. Pour all the egg mixture back into the saucepan with the milk-cream mixture and cook over medium-low heat, stirring constantly with a wooden spoon, until the foam on the top begins to subside and the custard is thick enough to coat the back of the spoon or reads 180°F. on an instant-read thermometer. Don't even think of not stirring. This takes only 15 to 20 minutes.

6. Immediately pour the mixture through the cheesecloth-lined sieve into the bowl and stir to bring the temperature down. Add the Fig Essence–port mixture and combine thoroughly. Chill in the refrigerator for a few hours and then freeze in an ice-cream maker according to the manufacturer's directions. When the ice cream is frozen, pack it into a freezer container and freeze 2 to 8 hours for its final "set" before serving.

MAKES ABOUT 1 QUART.

Mint Julep Ice Cream

*2 cups fresh peppermint leaves,
   rinsed and patted dry*
*2 cups high-quality bourbon, such
   as Maker's Mark, Jack
   Daniel's, or Jim Beam*

I. Remove any peppermint leaves that are turning black, as they will discolor the elixir. Using a mallet, rolling pin, or other heavy object, "bruise" the green leaves. Place them in a very clean mason jar, and pour the bourbon over them.

2. Cover the jar tightly and let steep for 24 hours, then strain through a cheesecloth-lined funnel into a very clean bottle or jar. Cover or cork tightly. Refrigeration is unnecessary.

Makes 2 cups.

This is best when timed so that the ice cream has set for two to eight hours before serving—the texture loses a little something on the following day.

¾ cup Mint Julep Elixir
7 egg yolks
¾ cup sugar
2 cups heavy cream
2 cups milk

1. Place the Mint Julep Elixir in a small saucepan, heat gently until barely simmering, and then simmer for 10 minutes.

2. Set a sieve lined with one layer of cheesecloth over a large bowl or pitcher. Keep handy.

3. Using an electric mixer, beat the egg yolks and sugar until thick and pale yellow—about 2 to 3 minutes.

4. Combine the cream and milk and scald in a heavy-bottomed saucepan. Add the Mint Julep Elixir to the cream mixture and heat to scalding again. Whisk about one-fourth of the cream mixture into the egg yolks, then pour all the egg yolk mixture back into the saucepan with the cream mixture. Stirring constantly with a wooden spoon, cook over low heat until the custard is thick enough to coat the back of the spoon or reads 180°F. on an instant-read thermometer. (Don't stop stirring or cook over too high a heat or the egg yolks may curdle.) This process takes about 20 minutes.

5. When the custard is thick, pour immediately through the sieve into the bowl or pitcher, stir a few times to bring the temperature down, and chill well. Freeze in an ice-cream maker according to manufacturer's directions. Pack into a freezer container and freeze for 2 to 8 hours for best consistency.

MAKES ABOUT 1 QUART.

Lemon-Ginger Cake

Ginger Oil

one 4-inch piece ginger root, peeled
and chopped into small dice
1 cup plus one teaspoon canola oil
or safflower oil

1. Combine the ginger and
the cup of oil in a saucepan
and warm gently for 10 to
12 minutes. Pour into a
very clean jar, let cool,
cover, and let steep in
the refrigerator for 24 to
48 hours.

2. Line a funnel with a
paper coffee filter and use
a pastry brush to paint the
filter with the remaining
teaspoon of oil. Pour the
Ginger Oil into the filter
and let it drip through the
funnel into another very
clean jar or bottle (this may
take some time). Cover or
cork tightly and label with
the date. Store refrigerated.

Makes about 1 cup.

Chiffon cakes are a perfect showcase for infused oils because they rely on oil rather than butter for their richness. This cake is especially lovely when surrounded by a combination of raspberries and blackberries.

2 cups unbleached all-purpose flour
1 cup sugar
½ teaspoon salt
2 teaspoons baking powder
½ cup fresh lemon juice
½ cup Ginger Oil
1 large egg yolk
6 egg whites
pinch of cream of tartar
Apricot Lemon Glaze (recipe follows)

1. Preheat the oven to 350°F.

2. Find an angel food cake pan or tube pan. Don't grease it.

3. In a large bowl, sift together the flour, sugar, salt, and baking powder, then whisk them to make sure they are well blended.

4. Mix together the lemon juice, ¼ cup water, the Ginger Oil, and the egg yolk and pour the mixture into the bowl with the dry ingredients. Do not mix yet.

5. Beat the egg whites with the cream of tartar until they hold stiff peaks. Quickly whisk the dry ingredients together with the wet ingredients. With a slotted spoon, add a healthy dollop of the beaten egg whites to the batter and

stir it in. Carefully fold in the remaining egg whites until there are no streaks left. Pour the batter into the angel food or tube pan and bake for 40 minutes.

6. Remove the pan from the oven, invert over a cake rack, and let cool, with the cake in the pan (this helps to keep the cake from settling—if it falls out, don't fret). Once the cake has cooled, remove it from the pan and place it on a cake rack for glazing.

Apricot Lemon Glaze

1 cup confectioners' sugar
2 tablespoons fresh lemon juice
2 teaspoons apricot jam

1. Sift the confectioners' sugar into a bowl and add the lemon juice and apricot jam. Mix well. Strain through a sieve to remove the stringy bits of apricot that sometimes appear in the jam.

2. Put the cake on a rack, with a sheet of wax paper or aluminum foil under the rack to catch the dripping glaze. Pour the glaze onto the cake, letting it dribble down the sides and into the center. Let the cake stand for an hour so the glaze can harden.

SERVES 10.

Variations:

Substitute Orange-Infused Oil (not to be confused with commercially available orange oil) or Lemon Herb Oil for the Ginger Oil. In either case, use orange juice in place of the lemon juice.

Mint Oil

2 ounces fresh mint (about 2 cups leaves), rinsed, patted dry, and allowed to air-dry thoroughly
1 cup plus 1 teaspoon canola oil or safflower oil

1. After discarding the larger stalks from the mint, combine the leaves and the cup of oil in a food processor or blender and process or blend for 10 seconds. Pour into a very clean jar, cover, and let steep in the refrigerator for 24 to 48 hours.

2. Line a funnel with a paper coffee filter and use a pastry brush to paint the filter with the remaining teaspoon of oil. Pour the Mint Oil into the filter and let it drip through the funnel into another very clean jar or bottle (this may take some time). Cover or cork tightly and label with the date. Store refrigerated.

Makes about 1 cup.

Chocolate-Mint Chiffon Cake

A friend's mother said that eating this cake was like eating a cold chocolate soufflé. The Ginger Oil version (see the Variation) is especially good with champagne.

dash of safflower oil or canola oil
½ cup sugar, plus extra for sprinkling in the pan
½ cup dark brown sugar, packed
1½ cups unbleached all-purpose flour
2 teaspoons baking powder
½ teaspoon salt
½ cup Dutch-processed cocoa powder
1 large egg yolk
½ cup Mint Oil
6 egg whites from large eggs (just over ¾ cup)
pinch of cream of tartar
Chocolate Mint Glaze (recipe follows)

1. Preheat the oven to 350°F.

2. Locate a 2-quart bundt pan. Lightly brush the inside of the pan with safflower oil and sprinkle sugar on the inside of the pan.

3. In a large bowl, whisk the ½ cup sugar and the brown sugar together until they are evenly distributed and blended. Sift the flour, baking powder, salt, and cocoa powder into the bowl with the sugars. Whisk all dry ingredients to blend. Make a well in the center and add the egg yolk, Mint Oil, and ¾ cup plus 1 tablespoon water. Do not mix.

Essential Flavors

4. In a separate bowl, with a clean electric beater or balloon hand whisk, beat the egg whites until foamy, then add the cream of tartar and beat until stiff.

5. Quickly blend the egg yolk, oil, and water into the dry ingredients.

6. Stir a healthy spoonful of beaten egg white into the chocolate mixture to lighten it. Fold the remaining egg whites into the chocolate mixture until there are no streaks left. Do not overfold. Pour the cake mixture into the bundt pan and put it in the oven. Bake for 35 to 40 minutes, or until the top springs back when touched and a cake tester inserted in the center of the cake comes out clean.

7. Cool in the pan for 1 hour. Remove the cake from the pan and cool on a cake rack. When cool, glaze with Chocolate Mint Glaze.

Chocolate Mint Glaze

4 ounces finest-quality bittersweet chocolate (we suggest Lindt Excellence), chopped
1 tablespoon Mint Oil
2 tablespoons heavy cream

1. Heat the chocolate in the top part of a double boiler over gently simmering water. When the chocolate has just barely melted (it may still look lumpy, but a quick stir will indicate whether or not it is indeed melted), remove from heat, whisk in the Mint Oil and cream, and stir until it has a glossy, creamy texture.

2. Put the cooled cake on a cake rack over a sheet of wax paper and spoon the glaze over it in ribbons, smoothing out the glaze with the back of a spoon. Scoop up the glaze that falls onto the wax paper and repour it. As it cools it should harden slightly.

SERVES 8 TO 10.

Variation:

Substitute Ginger Oil for the Mint Oil in both the cake and glaze recipes. With this substitution in the cake recipe, add 1 teaspoon powdered ginger to the cocoa. If you have some crystallized ginger on hand, chop it up and sprinkle it on top of the cake as a pretty garnish.

Essential Flavors

Vanilla-Rum Elixir Tea Cake

In this nutritionally correct age, there are times when we crave an egg-butter-sugar splurge, and this is the cake for those care-free moments. It's just as good with morning coffee as it is with afternoon tea—or after-dinner espresso, for that matter.

For the topping:
1½ cups shelled pecans
½ cup unbleached all-purpose flour
¾ cup dark brown sugar, packed
6 tablespoons unsalted butter, softened
pinch of salt
¼ cup Vanilla-Rum Elixir

For the cake:
1½ cups unbleached all-purpose flour
1 tablespoon baking powder
¼ teaspoon salt
⅓ cup Vanilla-Rum Elixir
⅓ cup milk
1 stick unsalted butter, softened, plus extra for greasing the pan
1 cup sugar
4 large eggs, separated
1 to 2 teaspoons confectioners' sugar, for finishing

1. Preheat the oven to 350°F.

2. Grease an 11- x 7-inch Pyrex baking dish.

Vanilla-Rum Elixir

2 cups golden rum, such as Mount Gay
4 vanilla beans

1. Pour the rum into a very clean jar. Split the vanilla beans lengthwise, scrape out the seeds in the center, and add the seeds to the rum. Cut the vanilla beans into 1-inch pieces and add to the rum. Let steep, covered, for 5 to 7 days.

2. Strain out the amount of elixir you need as you use it. Add replacement rum to the jar so that you always have some elixir on hand, steeping. You do not need to replace the vanilla beans each time, but you might want to add a new bean every other time you deplete your whole jar of elixir.

Makes 2 cups.

3. To make the topping: Combine pecans, flour, brown sugar, butter, and salt in the bowl of a food processor. Pulse several times, until the nuts are chopped and the ingredients combined. Drizzle in the Vanilla-Rum Elixir and pulse several more times to combine. Set aside.

4. To make the cake: Sift together the flour, baking powder, and salt.

5. In a small bowl, combine the Vanilla-Rum Elixir with the milk.

6. Cream the butter with an electric mixer. Add the sugar and cream it into the butter until it is combined. Add the egg yolks, beating until well combined. In three batches, add the flour mixture alternately with the elixir-milk mixture, for six additions in total. Begin with the flour and end with the liquid. Beat well after each dry and liquid addition, until well combined.

7. In a separate bowl with clean beaters, beat the egg whites until stiff peaks form. Add a dollop of the beaten whites into the cake batter and stir to combine. Working quickly, fold in the remaining egg whites with a slotted spoon or rubber spatula until the batter is uniform in color. Pour the batter into the prepared baking dish. Distribute the topping mixture as evenly as possible onto the cake batter, and don't worry if you don't get complete coverage.

8. Bake for 40 minutes, or until a cake tester inserted in the center comes out clean. Let cake cool in pan and dust lightly with a teaspoon or so of confectioners' sugar.

SERVES 8 TO 10.

INDEX